REVELATION OF LOVE

Scripture, Prayers and Reflections for Eucharistic Adoration

by
David Maria Turoldo

Edited by Espedito D'Agostini

With a Foreword by
Cardinal Silvano Piovanelli

BOOKS & MEDIA
BOSTON

Library of Congress Cataloging in Publication Data

Turaldo, David Maria, 1916-
 [Neanchè Dio può stare solo. English]
 Revelation of love : Scripture, prayers, and reflections for Eucharistic adoration / by David Maria Turoldo ; edited by Espedito D'Agostini ; with a foreword by Silvano Piovanelli.
    p. cm.
 Includes bibliographical references.
 ISBN 0-8198-6462-5 (pbk.)
 1. Lord's Supper—adoration—Prayer-books and devotions—English. 2. Catholic Church—Prayer-books and devotions—English. I. D'Agostini, Espedito. II. Title.
BX2233.T8713   1996
264'.02—dc20   96-33646
                                                              CIP

Quotations from the Book of Psalms taken from the HOLY BIBLE, NEW INTERNATIONAL VERSION. Copyright © 1973, 1978, 1984, International Bible Society. Used by permission of Zondervan Bible Publishers.

All other Scripture quotations contained herein are from the *Revised Standard Version Bible,* Catholic Edition, copyrighted 1965 and 1966 by the Division of Christian Education of the National Council of Churches of Christ in the U.S.A., and are used by permission. All rights reserved.

Special permission granted to use in this publication the 'you-your-yours' forms of personal pronoun in the address to God.

Original title: *Neanchè Dio può stare solo*

Copyright © 1991, Edizioni Piemme S.p.A., Via del Carmine 5, 15033, Casale Monferrato (AL), Italy

Translated from the Italian by Mary James Berger, FSP, and Sr. Mary Jeremiah Gillett, OP.

English edition copyright © 1996, Daughters of St. Paul

Printed and published in the U.S.A. by Pauline Books & Media, 50 St. Paul's Avenue, Boston, MA 02130.

Pauline Books & Media is the publishing house of the Daughters of St. Paul, an international congregation of women religious serving the Church with the communications media.

1 2 3 4 5   99 98 97 96

Contents

Foreword 7

Preface 11

Part I:
The Eucharist: Secret Aspiration of Humanity

An Invitation 17

And There We Celebrate the Nuptial Banquet 33

Part II:
"Only One Desire Consumes Me:
To Eat This Passover with You"

The Plan of These Celebrations 37

1. The Lord's Supper 43

2. Do This in Memory of Me 51

3. The Bread of Life 59

4. The Blood of the New and Perfect Covenant 67

5. Eucharist: Revelation of Love 75

6. Eucharist: Mystery of Communion 83

7. Eucharist: Language of the Inexpressible 91

8. Eucharist: Presence of the Invisible 99

9. Eucharist: Living in Praise 109

10. Eucharist: Living in Peace 117

11. Eucharist: Living in Expectation 125

12. Eucharist: Essence of Creation 133

13. Eucharist: Sacrifice for Life 141

14. Eucharist: Calming of Every Desire 149

15. Eucharist: "Place" of Communion 157

16. Eucharist: Perfection of the Saints 165

17. Eucharist: Proclamation of Transfiguration 173

18. Eucharist: Proclamation of Glory 181

Notes 189

Foreword

Two motives impelled me to accept Father David's request to write a foreword for this book. The first—in order of time and importance—is friendship. One cannot say "no" to a friend. The second is gratitude.

I want to say thanks to Father David for these pages, which he defines as an "invitation and an aid to prayer" for Eucharistic adoration.

This book can help us respond to the call of Pope John Paul II, expressed in his 1980 Holy Thursday letter to priests: "The adoration of Christ in this sacrament of love must find its expression in various forms of Eucharistic devotion. The animation and deepening of Eucharistic worship are a proof of that authentic renewal which the Council proposed as its goal and which are at its center.... Jesus awaits us in this sacrament of love. Let us not economize on the time we take to meet him in adoration and in the full contemplation of faith."

The following reflection of Father Raniero Cantalamessa impresses me: "Eucharistic piety is a gift the Holy Spirit has made to the Catholic Church. The Church must cultivate this gift with gratitude....

"In Christianity, every great spiritual current has had its own particular charism, which constitutes its contribution to the wealth of the whole Church. For Protestants, it is the veneration of the Word of God; for the Orthodox, the veneration of icons; for Catholics, the worship of the Eucharist.

"Through each of these three ways, the same basic aim is fulfilled—the contemplation of Christ and of his mystery. If the particular gift of the Catholic Church and the secret of its strength lies in the unique manner in which the Eucharistic Jesus is present and adored in the Church, then we see how important it is that we value this gift fully once more."

Many adults are returning to personal and communal adoration of the Eucharist. Living and devout participation in the liturgy helps them reflect more on the great Gift of the Presence and makes their contemplation more enlightened and profound.

Some young people, too, feel the need to remain at the feet of the Master, as did Mary of Bethany, to listen to his words and meditate on them in their hearts, or simply to look upon him with eyes of faith, in the joyful awareness that it is always he who first gazes lovingly on us.

If in meditation the loving search for truth prevails, in contemplation we have the loving enjoyment of truth found.

If, on the one hand, we recount to the Father what Jesus has done for us, on the other, we recount for ourselves his gestures and words so as to be able to walk in his footsteps.

The Church has taken to heart many commitments. Her presence is requested from all sides. She rightly strives to respond to the history that challenges her. But, in the end—to live the communion that comes from God and to communicate to all people the

Foreword

gift of reconciliation—the Church must measure everything by the Eucharist.

If the Mass is the vigorous and inexhaustible source of the life that is Christ himself, then the time spent in adoration—enriched and deepened with the help of this precious book—is like the hours after an abundant rainfall, when the water slowly penetrates and thoroughly soaks the earth.

An example of such prayer was habitually given by Giorgio La Pira. His thanksgivings after Communion were never rushed, and his frequent, solitary adorations were not timed. From this adoration of the Eucharist sprang the dynamism of his actions, always rich in faith, charged with prophecy, open in charity to the service of the poor, to his political commitments, to universal peace.

When Moses came down from Mount Sinai after conversing with God, his skin had become radiant, even though he was unaware of it.

Every disciple who climbs the mount of Eucharistic contemplation returns radiant, even if unaware. He returns to human companionship, happy that God is among us—Emmanuel. He returns committed to reflecting this presence of love in openness and service.

Here then is my wish and prayer: may this book help many persons radiate the Eucharist!

Cardinal Silvano Piovanelli
Archbishop of Florence

Preface

Prayer is a difficult and endless undertaking, because after having learned how to pray—and we cannot avoid placing ourselves in the school of the Master who prays (cf. Lk 11:1)—we run the risk of falling into commonplace, repetitive, wasteful words (cf. Mt 6:7-8). It is a matter of reaching a dialogue between God and the person—of listening to the Word and responding with word and song (cf. SC 33)—taking part in that dialogue which Christ inaugurated with the Father in the power of the Spirit and which his disciples are exhorted to pursue with perseverance and continuity. The prayer of contemplation is more difficult, for it penetrates the mystery of God, sounds its depths, looks into his image, as into a mirror, and welcomes the reflection so as to transform our passing days and give them meaning.

For these reasons, without downplaying the value of a theoretical treatise (we find many right from the beginning—to speak only of the Church in Africa—from Tertullian to Cyprian and Augustine), an aid to "lived" prayer seems particularly useful. Prayer, like faith, needs to be "spoken" in the daily experience of every age, of every culture. And like faith, of which it is an expression, it needs to be "spoken" with dignity, truth and, if possible, beauty.

Without doubt, a book of prayer in which the pen and interior passion of Father David Maria Turoldo are evident, has the merit of dignity and beauty, because of its poetry. In addition we have here the experience of a community which has prayed together for about thirty years—which has built its fraternal life on the prayer of listening, contemplation, internalization, praise, supplication, intercession and, above all, song. With discretion and joy, this community now offers its experience as a fraternal help, because it is beautiful and right to communicate the gifts of God to our brothers and sisters. To help others to pray with dignity and in beauty: what greater service could we render to our Church today, which in its liturgy seems sometimes to forget to artistically combine the beautiful and the true?

The special value of this book consists in the focusing of prayer on the Eucharistic mystery. This is more than prayer around or before the Eucharist. This prayer begins with the Eucharistic mystery, with the very celebration of it, so as to grasp all its dimensions, contemplate its bottomless depths and draw implications for life. This guide goes to the heart of the Christian faith—a risky action which seems to have succeeded, with promising benefit for Eucharistic piety and—not a small point—ecumenical dialogue.

Despite its subtitle and the well-ordered outline for each celebration, *Revelation of Love* is not intended for a specific or obligatory use. It is presented as an "open" instrument for contemplative prayer based on the Eucharistic mystery and uses a variety and wealth of themes according to a methodology that is as precious as it is rare. In fact, the almost thousand-year separation of

Eucharistic "celebration" and "worship" has been overcome—a separation that was one of the causes of controversy with the Protestant Reformation and of the doctrinal impoverishment of Eucharistic devotion. At the same time, the text recovers those rich dimensions of faith proper to the celebration and re-presents them with inspired literary figures (hymn, response, communion song...) for contemplative prayer.*

Eucharistic worship arose in an age that was not very rich in Eucharistic theology and praxis; the first was reduced to a theology of the Presence and the second to a rite closed to the understanding and participation of the Christian people. Devotion was quickly separated from Eucharistic celebration, in which it had grown as an autonomous element, losing not only the integrity of the faith-perspective but also its ecclesial, communal purpose. Though rich in forms and exterior solemnity, the hymns and prayers that accompanied its development do not go beyond the reaffirmation of objective faith and the refutation of heresy. The best hymns, in Latin, all belong to the thirteenth century and come, for the most part, from communion prayers.

After Vatican II, along with the renewed Eucharistic theology and full participation of the Christian people, there was a re-centralization of worship that drew its origin from the Eucharistic mystery and led back to it. The practice of recent years has not always been faithful to the spirit of the postconciliar documents (from *Eucharisticum Mysterium* of 1967 to *Dominicae Cenae* and *Inaestimabile Donum* of 1980). But the journey is irreversible and its fruits are manifest in this publication, in which the series of prayer themes present a linear theological course on all the values that constitute the real dimensions of the Eucharist—from human language to the content of faith, from the time of institution to the time of the eschaton, from the aspect of banquet to that of Church, from divine love's revelation to its response; above all, from the contemplation of the celebration to the living out of daily reality. It is a Eucharist opened up to all existence—to the whole history of yesterday, today and tomorrow, from the encounter under the signs of a meal to full communion and the building up of the praying community into the living Body of Christ.

In short, the text documents prayer made with dignity but also in truth, in the truth of a genuine, substantial faith, expressed especially in the opening hymn and the song of communion (two important elements, together with the praise of Mary) which unite the hearts and voices of the praying community. It is a healthy and complete Eucharistic theology transformed into a community prayer that seeks to penetrate the mystery and participate in it with fervor. Other communities can draw inspiration from this.

Rinaldo Falsini, OFM

It has not been possible to translate the beautiful hymns of the original Italian edition into rhythmical, meaningful English—Ed.

Part I
The Eucharist: Secret Aspiration of Humanity

An Invitation

This book is meant to be an invitation and an aid to prayer. But there is nothing better than "going beyond." May persons and communities compose their own prayers, for they are led by the Spirit to penetrate those areas which the liturgy—of its nature universal (the greatest gift the Spirit has made to the Church)—leaves open to creativity and the fulfillment of particular needs in various times and places. From one part of the earth to the other, there is a compelling ontological and structural need to sing together the common song and to pray the same prayer, so as never to feel alone, excluded from the communion of saints. The unity of humanity is a sign and revelation of the unity of God.

This is the most delicate and decisive moment for the universality and unity of the Church and of the world, a universality and unity that must be confessed by the unity of faith: "all filled with the one bread, joined in the same prayer." Because the body is one, one is our faith. "There is one body and one Spirit...one God and Father of us all, who is above all and through all and in all" (Eph 4:4-6). This is part of the irresistible design of the Spirit, who never says anything on his own but draws everything from Christ, the one Lord of history, and who breathes to and fro where he wills, bringing creativity and freedom everywhere.

Two necessities are rooted in these premises: to feel ourselves within the universal tradition as within the river of life, and at the same time to be more and more fully ourselves, ever new revelations of God, each one of us a new song of creation, an unmistakable and irrepressible note in the general chorus. This allows us to express life and history—that is, to be both faithful and free.

This book is a small instrument, nothing more, and an invitation. It is meant to help all of us rediscover our taste for praying, singing and contemplating. May great song and great joy flourish in our liturgies, and may beauty return to our assemblies!

We cannot help, then, but begin from the very heart of worship, from this heart of the world which is the Eucharist. All life ends in eucharist. The Eucharist is the *entelechy*—the total actuality, par excellence. It is a sign of the purpose and end of all creation. Everything seeks a eucharist; it is through the Eucharist that existence touches and enters into being; it is in the Eucharist that love finds its true expression; through it God's solitude and ours are forever overcome in a unique and marvelous way. Through it we communicate with all creatures, and death is defeated.

We cannot begin except from here: it is the mystery of the *Shekinah* that is perpetuated in the history of the world. It was symbolized by the *Shekinah* in the *Holy of Holies* of the Temple, or by the Ark that was God's dwelling place in the midst of the people journeying through the desert.

In addition to the hymns, in which I sought to grasp the mystery, light from light, I have included some reflections that I believe can nurture our understanding that a community can never prescind from the Eucharist—that the contemplation of this sacrament is indispensable for attaining the most dreamed-of ideals. Life itself wants to become eucharist. And so—to achieve the perfect covenant and realize full communion; to live peace; to live in expectation of the reconciliation of every desire, in the hope of transfiguration—these are only some of the eighteen themes proposed, always through the mystery of his Body, the substance of creation and, beneath every appearance, the supreme gift of Being.

In the beginning, therefore, the Eucharist!

If only we could take it seriously! This is the heart of the Church, the center of gravity of the world and of history; this is the passageway to the Eternal. And there is only silence. A small host—even smaller than the ark which contained the staff of Moses and the book of the law. A host that says nothing, that has no taste or smell. And yet, if it were in only one place on earth, the whole earth—as the *Imitation of Christ* says—would gravitate toward that place, drawn by the Eucharist's mysterious force of attraction. (All the truths of God are like that, as is God himself, beginning with his name. Therefore we must not use his name too lightly: at the mere sound of that name, time and the stars should halt and the sea should hold its breath.)

And instead we talk and talk and become agitated; we organize a din and an uproar around that name and sacrament, the sacrament of silence that corresponds to the infinite silence of God. We cultivate devotions without end, and adapt them, and prepare countless ceremonies, which may even be idolatrous profanations, although not intentionally so.

And Christ never says anything. We break the host and it

does not react. We should see it bleeding, as the eucharist of Archbishop Oscar Romero bled, to the point that he was killed with the chalice in his hand, after having said: "This chalice contains the wine that is about to become the blood [of Christ]." Oscar Romero, bishop for the people, what were your masses like? In that cathedral which exploded with the songs of an entire populace who came every Sunday to celebrate Christ and their deceased, in that sole reality that was the highest point of their lives, the Eucharist, how were your Eucharistic celebrations?

We, for our part, celebrate almost as an escape from our existential responsibilities, whether individual or social. Sometimes we go to celebrate because we don't know what else to do, or because we don't want to commit ourselves. This is exactly the opposite of what the Eucharist signifies. Our celebrations are often as stern and sterilized as morgues! Or they are elaborate ceremonies that mean nothing. And so nothing ever happens. None of us is killed, while we commemorate the One who was killed by the whole world, the victim who continues to be killed. Theology itself tells us, "nothing in the history of the world is so revolutionary as to celebrate the Eucharist," this celebrating the memory (that is, living) the passion, death and resurrection of Christ! This celebration says, in effect, that the cause of humanity continues and no one can stop it.

Eucharist and community

I want to speak of Eucharist and community. Naturally I will speak softly; these are very delicate truths and it takes little to ruin them; they lie at the heart of the mystery.

When we consider Eucharist and then community, we at once ask ourselves whether they are not two truths called to form, to actualize, one sole reality. It is difficult, if not impossible, to think of Eucharist without a community, even as it would be difficult, if not impossible, to think of a community without Eucharist.

We can neither make nor have community without sacrifice. For now let us accept the terms in their broad, all-inclusive meaning—in an analogical and even an anagogical sense. That each community requires gift and offering will be seen even more clearly further on.

So, are community and Eucharist two realities or only one? Speaking for now only in the area of faith, we do not have Eucharist without community, as we do not have community without Eucharist. Community is an essential dimension of the human person: no one lives by or for self alone. The Eucharist is the communal event par excellence: it comes into being as a meal for the multitudes, with the aim of inaugurating the kingdom that will come at the end time—a sign of the eternal banquet. In fact, the Eucharist is offered as a goal of life and a seed of eternity: "those who feed on my flesh have eternal life" (cf. Jn 6:54). And so the Eucharist is placed between time and eternity, between the present life and the next, as the sole future of earthly life. Not by chance is it a participation in the passion, death and resurrection of the Lord. This is mystery—not because we don't understand anything at all, but because the complete truth transcends our grasp.

Only one reality

We may express it this way: Eucharist and community are two aspects of only one reality, as reciprocal cause and effect. As the soul gives life to the body, so the Eucharist gives life to community. Without the spirit there is no human person (at most we would have a "carnal person," unable to perceive the things of the Spirit). And without a body there is no spirit, or at least we cannot know how and what spirit is; the body gives visibility to the invisible. (For these reasons we should speak of the body with stronger conviction; without a body, without material creation, we can't even discuss God; light is invisible without something to reveal it. The body is God's glory, his manifestation, his epiphany.)

Without community we do not celebrate Eucharist; without community we do not render visible any of the creative and saving love of God on earth. Everything is consummated in community. Community is the existential realization of the Eucharist as regards the subject, and its historical realization as regards the object. No community is built if not around a word. (Analogously, this is true for associations, too; they come into being around a program.) With greater reason this happens around the Word of God. Not by chance do we call it the "living Word." The Word of God is food and drink, necessary nourishment for the body, and the body is the community.

We can say that for the same reasons—that is, for the reasons inherent in the nature of the Word of life become flesh—this Word cannot but yearn to become food and drink, to be consumed— precisely so as to achieve the purpose for which the Word took to himself a body. The Word became incarnate as a man; he made himself visible. Christ became one of us, even though in his assumption of human nature he carries within himself the principle of universality. The text says: "The Word became flesh and dwelt *among* us" (Jn 1:14).

Through his incarnation Christ has become one *of* us, while through the Eucharist he becomes one *with* us, both individually and collectively. He becomes a multitude, even in the physical sense; he becomes a people, a "dynamic" of humanity: "You shall be my people, and I will be your God" (Jer 30:22). And so it becomes evident that the Eucharist is the true fulfillment of the incarnation and at the same time its perpetuation in time. Thus, the Eucharist continues to become Church. It is the true "All has been fulfilled" of Christ (cf. Jn 19:30), insofar as it is the total giving of his whole life. We can also say that through the incarnation the Father gave the Son to the world; with the Eucharist it is the Son who gives himself. He makes us participants, in time, of his resurrection—that is, participants in his whole temporal and glorious life. Finally, the mystery joins us with eternity, so that we too might overcome death in ourselves.

(Eucharistic Communion is a nourishing of oneself with the divinity, so as to save oneself from solitude, from desperation, from death. For this reason the Eucharist is a universal event for the human condition, and its traces can be found among all peoples. It forms part of *eros,* the mysterious love-force of all humanity. The lover says to the loved one: "I love you so much that I could 'eat you up.'" That is not possible for human love, but it *is* possible for divine love, since it is the only infinite love.)

The purpose of creation

This is how Christ explained his state of soul: "With what longing have I longed" (cf. Lk 22:15). I burn with longing, I cannot wait; I have looked forward to nothing but "this hour" my whole life. Now the time has come, the supreme moment of love.

The Eucharist is a compendium of the whole life of Christ. In fact, it is Christ himself; and nothing else. Above all, it is not a "holy thing" leading us into unconscious idolatry.

Since the whole life of Christ is in the Eucharist, the whole plan of God is also there. In the Eucharist, the purpose of creation and of the incarnation is fulfilled; in it is born the Church, the community that is a figure of the kingdom to come. For those who believe, the Eucharist is the ultimate goal of history. Not by chance is it consumed in the form of a banquet, of a wedding feast: "Come to the marriage feast" (Mt 22:4) or "I tell you, not one of those men who were invited shall taste my banquet!" (Lk 14:24). The latter persons addressed do not form part of the body, do not form themselves in love. Therefore they will have no part in the kingdom. It is the Eucharist that judges us individually, and also judges the Church itself: whether the Church is a real community, whether it is a true image of the kingdom.

The Eucharist is the "everything" that is "accomplished" (cf. Jn 19:30), both in our self-gift and in God's. God lets himself be eaten, and we eat, so that everyone should say: "It is no longer I who live, but Christ who lives in me" (Gal 2:20). Yes, it is God who is consumed, who disappears within us. This self-giving love becomes the source of unity for the world, overcoming all egoism, knocking down all barriers. In the Eucharist the work of the Father is completed. From the beginning he wanted to make a covenant with all humanity; now at last, the kingdom of God is realized!

In the Eucharist the work of the Son is completed, for this is the last gesture of Christ in God: "Take and eat me, for I want to remain in you forever, so that you may live of me who have conquered death, and you may have everlasting life." In fact, to live the Eucharist in all its fullness (if we succeed in doing so!) means to already be in the kingdom. A saint prayed this way: "Lord, on the day that I achieve a true and perfect Communion, with all that it comprehends and involves, take me to yourself, for I will already be in your kingdom." But when can we say that we have accomplished a perfect Eucharist?

An Invitation

The ultimate goal of the Holy Spirit is that this Eucharist be realized—that full community be achieved, a true Church; that cosmic communion, the plan of all creation, be fulfilled. Everything tends toward unity. We can never repeat often enough that the purpose of history is for the whole human race to be formed in love, for all creatures to be joined together in peace, for the "groaning of creation" to come to an end.

Not by chance is the Eucharist eaten. It is in eating and being eaten that full identity is reached between things and the conscious human being. It is by being eaten that things truly become me and I become their consciousness. And so even God becomes me, and I establish myself in him, and through me, God establishes himself in all creation. Then the whole earth can be called the Lord's host, Christ's body. This is where creatures finally attain communion, physical contact with their Lord: "Eucharist, the sacrament of unity and peace for the entire universe."

The Eucharist is the only reason that the other sacraments exist. It is the first reason for the existence of family life, as a *beginning* of the prophecy of the kingdom. In fact, the loving married couple constitute the first visible sign of love between God and humanity.

The Eucharist is also the first reason for the existence of religious life, which is the *fulfillment* of the prophecy of the kingdom: a sign of the time when there will no longer be man or woman, for we will all be united in the One. Religious life is a proclamation of the end of the ages.

Not by chance is this already found in the heart of each Eucharistic Prayer, both before and after the transubstantiation:

"Father, accept this offering *for your whole family*. Grant us your peace in this life..." (I).

"May all of us who share in the body and blood of Christ *be brought together in unity...*" (II).

"Grant that we, who are nourished by his body and blood, may be filled with his Holy Spirit, and become one body, one spirit in Christ.... Lord, may this sacrifice, which has made our peace with you, advance the *peace and salvation of all the world*" (III).

"...gather all...*into the one body of Christ,* a living sacrifice of praise" (IV).

The unity of the sacraments

The goal of all the sacraments is the Eucharist, precisely in the sense of communion with God, with our brothers and sisters and with all creation. (In his *Canticle of the Creatures,* St. Francis celebrates an authentic Eucharistic prayer, of cosmic proportions.)

Baptism makes us all children of God, members of one family. Even my father is my brother, since he was baptized as I was; even the Pope is my brother, although the first among brothers.

Confirmation definitively makes us temples of the Holy Spirit (cf. 1 Cor 3:17): a "divine edifice"; a church or living Pentecost!

Penance, or *metanoia,* which means conversion, is also called the sacrament of reconciliation, for through it we are all restored to a state of communion, not only the penitent with us, but we with the penitent.

In Christian Marriage, the spouses love one another in expectation of more who will love one another, and in expectation that all of us will love one another.

Holy Orders is the sacrament that anoints a man for the service of the community.

In the Sacrament of the Sick, bodies are anointed and perfumed for the kingdom.

Everything leads to the ultimate reality: the Eucharist as Viaticum or as the farewell supper, a premise and promise "until we all meet again at the eternal wedding banquet." Meanwhile, as we pray, "When we eat this bread and drink this cup, we proclaim your death, Lord Jesus, until you come in glory," we are both here and there at the same time.

Just so, at a suitable point in the rite, the existential discourse is suspended so as to enter into the event that was accomplished once and for always—an absolute and unrepeatable event, almost as though history stopped "on the night on which he was betrayed," which is the great night of the world. When we leave behind our daily becoming to perpetuate the event of that night, the "Lord's death until he comes" (1 Cor 11:26) is made real and present and contemporary. It diffuses itself spiritually throughout the world to sanctify every death experienced for love, every life that is immolated. Through it everything is redeemed, every struggle for liberation is blessed: liberation from other humans, from personal sin and from the sin of the world: "Lamb of God you take away the sin of the world."

Through this "fixed point" of human history, this void in time, we enter into the unique and immovable event which is the mysterious heart of that history, a heart that beats until its last drop of blood is shed. In the same way, by God's breaking into time, through the unity of the whole life of Christ who gives himself in the Eucharist, we are called to participate in his resurrection. Definitive death no longer exists; the life of the Christian is already a risen life, a life projected beyond death, a life charged with immortality even in time. Such must be the life of the Church, against which "the powers of death shall not prevail" (Mt 16:18). Such is the testimony of the martyrs. Such in our own times was the testimony of Oscar Romero, who said, "Once I am killed, I will rise again in my people." It is not only a question of the final resurrection, but of an anticipated resurrection: "being already present" on the part of the saints, who not only eat but "are eaten," who are living, present and active.

This is the Eucharist, a bridge between the community and the kingdom, between the Church on the move and "the holy city coming down from heaven," beautiful as a spouse ready for her wedding. Eucharist—living in the kingdom, if it is true eucharist.

Forced march toward the unity of the world

At this point we should widen our horizons and move beyond the boundaries of our faith—to take up and develop those allusions already made above that the eucharistic phenomenon is universal, verifiable in all religions. Eucharist is a profound secret in the history of peoples.

The whole world seeks unity. Throughout the world there is a mysterious eucharist—a need to build unity with everyone, to be one community. For this reason everyone seeks the "same thing." Someone has even written about the most recent ideologies: "communism or communion." And others have said of the modern city: "either an anthill or an agàpe." Chesterton said that the dominant ideologies today are nothing other than Christian truths gone mad. On the same topic Berdjaev wrote: "Marxism is nothing other than a punch given to an unfulfilled Christianity." Cardinal Suhard, too, in one of the most important postwar pastoral letters, *Agony of the Church,* stated that the world is "on a forced march toward unity," and he asked: "What does this unity entail and by whom will it be realized?" That is, by wars and genocide or by ecumenicity?

In the Bible the human person is presented as having three dimensions: cosmic, communal and divine. A human being is the sum of all creation: earth that cries out and adores or blasphemes. We speak of the microcosm that reflects the macrocosm. And yet,

"It is not good that the man should be alone" (Gen 2:18). A person needs completeness, needs to expand into a "you" that is likewise conscious, in order to achieve a "we" that expresses free and necessary harmony. The harmony of created things is already a prophetic, though unconscious, sign of this harmony. It is in human awareness that the existence of material things and even the being of God take on meaning and reason. Humanity is the conscious point of the unity of the whole cosmos, both of matter and of spirit. And this truth acquires concreteness when we discover love, the uniting power of all reality. When persons love and give themselves and make peace, then they are the image and revelation of God; they are actualizing their being in its fullness and mystery.

For this purpose God "created man in his own image, in the image of God he created him; male and female he created them" (Gen 1:27), that they might be his manifestation: "No man has ever seen God; if we love one another, God abides in us and his love is perfected in us" (1 Jn 4:12). Here the ultimate reality of the world is consummated, when we make ourselves a living eucharist—awareness of cosmic unity, of universal community, of the continual manifestation of God. Then the world achieves its purpose; it attains the peace of God that surpasses all understanding. This is the motivating plan, the purpose woven throughout the texture of the world's history. This explains even politics; as crazy and absurd as politics may be, it seeks the unity of the human race, even if by means of massacres.

The community, the Church, the unity of the human race, the final coming of the kingdom: all these guide God in his work, from creation to the Eucharist. And this will be life's conclusion: "Come, you blessed of my Father, inherit the kingdom prepared for you from the foundation of the world" (Mt 25:34), an inheritance promised and attached only to the act of love, the unique, true content of the Eucharist, or to communion with God in the gift of self to our brothers and sisters.

"Do this in remembrance of me" (Lk 22:19) is not only the foundation of a mandate for the ministerial priesthood. It traces a program of life: "As I have done for you so are you to do for each other; only in this way will you truly celebrate my memory" (cf. Jn 13:14-15).

Not by chance did St. Paul center his whole theology on what he "received from the Lord" (1 Cor 11:23) and handed on to the churches—that is, the Eucharist. And he made a rich synthesis of his whole message by defining Christians as those who "speak the truth in love," *én agàpe,* (cf. Eph 4:15)—a condition always expressed in the present participle, thus saying that only agàpe is the realization of God in us.

Here the Eucharist completes its insertion into the aspirations of all peoples: a response to every communal symbol that exists in the world, not only the rites of holy meals, of "sacred banquets," but also the eager relationship of lovers who remain—in the framework of symbol—more and more hungry and disappointed, having "more hunger after the meal than before."

Herein lies the grave responsibility and great mission of the Church: to become a living eucharist.

This concerns all humanity, since all burn with the same longing.

And for those who do not believe?

How can others be interested in our discussion if they know nothing of Christ or Christianity or the Eucharist, and even say that they have no faith at all?

I think St. Augustine had a similar problem in mind when he

made the following distinctions regarding the Eucharist. He says (I will quote the thought in Latin first, so as not to lose the strength of what he wanted to express): *"Sunt qui manducant sed non manducantur."* There are people who eat but are not eaten. Who are they? Am I perhaps one of them? Are they those who practice but don't believe? Are they those whose belief is lukewarm? Certainly, they are inconstant: they are persons without the "torment" of God.

"Sunt qui non manducant sed manducantur." These are people who do not eat but are eaten. And who are they? People who seek, who burn with longing. They are people who do not practice religion but want to believe, to the point of torment. They are "eaten" by God.

"Sunt qui manducant et manducantur." These are people who eat and are eaten. We can identify them immediately. They are the holy and just of the world. Their condition is the ideal.

So then, not even strangers (I never say "atheists") are so alien as not to have some relation with this sacrament. Not by chance is the Eucharist defined as the "mystery of faith."

Still and always the same mass for the world

Let us speed up now and roam through heaven and earth with the soul of Teilhard de Chardin, who dreamed of nothing other than the living unity of the world. This was his mass, his priesthood, his science at the service of all creation "that ascended and awaited"—of creation that still ascends and awaits, since everything is in act, everything is co-present. God is always contemporary, and he "draws everything to himself with his will." Cosmogenesis, biogenesis, noogenesis are always in view of Christo-genesis. And this is to be our eucharist for the world, without forgetting anything or anyone, not a day of our history, not a single person, for we are all "sick (with longing) for God," and are all to find fulfillment in him. So like Christ let us open our arms on the mount and not forget anyone.

In the end, to respond to the goodness of this total gift of God, we can do nothing better than what St. Thomas Aquinas did. After having composed the *Summa Theologica,* the greatest cathedral raised by human genius to the Godhead and to creation, even Thomas could do nothing other than to cover his mouth and keep silent (cf. Job 40:4-5). Here everything fails—intellect and senses—everything is shipwrecked in the sea of love. So we, too, can do nothing else but abandon ourselves to this love and sing: "I adore you, hidden God."

And There We Celebrate the Nuptial Banquet

Will There Ever Be a Seventh Day?

Speak to us, O God, of your endless labor:
suspicions about it are even now being whispered.
Are you, too—infinitely more than we—
without rest?

A dream may even urge you on
to transcend the boundaries of your solitude,
a dream that makes even inanimate things wakeful!

There the nuptial banquet is celebrated,
sharing the Bread and the Wine that has become blood;
and in complete actualization
the two expectations are appeased,
since we, too, are forbidden to cross over the abyss.

Divine passion breaks the cycle of nature.
The Word infinitely resounds
from your mouth—another you,
and between both of you breathes
the common Spirit, the vortex of Love,

which at once delights and torments:
the first Fire, origin of every other fire
that in the infinity
of other flames expands....

And so, God, you cannot but create:
peopling the expanses of stars,
filling the abyss of Nothing.
And then you deceive yourself
that you will make man
into a successful image of yourself!

"Shadow of the Dream"—hardly a shield!

However, if such a consciousness
did not mirror you, and the infinite
number of beings did not at least reflect
flashes of you,
you would never have a meaning:
you too would be lost and without glory.

Nor can we say that you created
only in the beginning,
since from that moment
if you should stop thinking of your creatures
for even an instant
and withdraw your breath from them,
Nothingness would swallow us up.

At least chain Nothingness, O God!
And overcome Evil,
the violation of the universe....

But since you cannot
but freely respect the rules,
you too are a God in suffering;
and we, the tragedy of your being God.

Part II

"Only One Desire Consumes Me: To Eat This Passover with You"

The Plan of These Celebrations

This aid for prayer-contemplation of the Eucharist aims to open some means of access to the great mystery which, together with the Word, constitutes the essential nucleus of the believer's whole life in Jesus Christ.

The fundamental criterion that has guided us in formulating these themes has been to draw complete attention to the Eucharistic presence of the Lord, arousing not only recognition of the real Presence on the part of the one praying but also and inseparably recognition of Christ's indwelling in the person whom he nourishes with his body and blood.

Therefore, while we contemplate one of the aspects of the Eucharistic mystery (memorial, communion, fullness of love) prayer sheds light on its effect and efficacy with regard to the believer as a person and as part of the community that is created around the table of the Lord.

There are eighteen outlines for this prayerful contemplation. The number stems from the relationship between six and three. Six recalls the hexameron, the days of creation, the number indicating mediation between the source and its manifestation. According to ancient cosmologies, six is also the number of spatial directions: the four cardinal points plus zenith and nadir. The number six also composes a star, shaped by the union of two triangles. The triangle with its vertex on top is a symbol of the divine nature of Christ, while the one with the vertex on the bottom refers to his human nature. The resulting six-pointed star depicts the union of the two natures.

Three has always been considered a fundamental number, indicating absolute perfection, without duality and ambivalence. On an anthropological level, it indicates an intellectual and spiritual order to which human beings aspire, in nostalgia for a harmonic principle that has been lost and is sought.

The number three is also understood as a symbol of unity, of an infinitely perfect synthesis: the result of joining one, heaven, and two, the earth.

And so even the number of our outlines carries a Eucharistic message: we relive a creative experience that concerns the whole cosmos. We are immersed in the initial fervor of life. We are caught up by the light that emanates from this mystery, as from the apparition of a splendid star, and led to the heart of the unifying work accomplished by Christ. We can approach the immense perfection of the love of God and draw from it a strength that may lead us to the knowledge of ourselves, beginning from God's self-revelation. This strength may give a balanced fulfillment to all our potentials to the point of becoming "perfect as the Father is perfect."

Omitting Sunday—the day of the Lord, privileged memorial of his Passover—these outlines ideally cover six days a week for three weeks, to indicate that all our time, our entire existence, in this "favorable moment" of life, must be experienced in the light of the mystery of the Son of God made man, as a "memory-action" of grace (Eucharist) of the marvels God has wrought for our salvation. This "favorable moment" is a necessary space in which we celebrate in truth and concreteness the incarnation and outpouring of blood in the one, eternal and universal offering of Christ Jesus. We "carry within us the fullness of joy," that is, awareness of an ever clearer and more complete adhesion with the one creative will.

Each outline has these essential elements, which can be adapted or amplified, according to the opportunities and circumstances in which they are used:

—A *brief introduction*. This may help the users to enter into a climate of listening and contemplation.

—An *invitation to prayer*—verses of a dialogue between the leader (v.) and the group *(r.)*. They are generally taken from psalms, prayers which Jesus used or referred to in marking the more decisive moments of his earthly life. These verses are intended to move the whole self to cross the threshold of the mystery in order to become immersed in it and yield to its fascination.

—An *entrance hymn*. By uniting our voices in one melody, this song helps us to be aware that we are only one body. The hymn opens our minds and frees our hearts to welcome the Word of God.

—A *prayer* before the readings. With this, the leader expresses the desire that God's Word may accomplish what it says. And everyone responds, Amen!

—The *first reading*. This is taken from a New Testament passage, understood as a witness to the new covenant, and as the first Christian community's gathering about the invisible presence of Christ.

—After a brief period of silence, the singing of a *psalm* impresses on the heart of the believer the fidelity of God's Word and the Lord's continuing work in history, according to the eternal plan of salvation for each of us and for all creation.

—As long as time exists, the reading of the *Gospel* constitutes the perennial proclamation of the good news for us, so that we may live of it and by it all the days of our lives.

—At this point a *third reading* has been inserted—a reflection on the theme of the celebration. It is not a commentary on the biblical readings, but a path for the spiritual "realization" of what we derive from the contemplation of the Eucharistic mystery, according to the designated theme.

—*Response.* This repetitive dialogue condenses the sentiments which have been aroused by what has been "seen and heard."

—*Intercessory prayers.* After the Word has been heard and welcomed, we pray that what God wills may take place, and that, moved by the Spirit, the whole people of God may manifest the Word's power.

—*Song of communion.* Before closing this prayer encounter, the faithful express with a hymn the reality of communion with the Eucharistic mystery which they have lived. This is the song of pilgrims on their journey, their hearts and eyes filled with the joyous vision, moving toward the encounter that has no end.

—*Praise of Mary.* It seemed fitting to include a final greeting to the Mother of God, she who gave to the world the Giver of life. She is the first faithful servant, who made her whole being, not only her body, the welcoming womb for the "Word made flesh." Admitted into the joy of perfect communion with the Trinity, she is the first fruits and sign of what we will be.

These steps form a sufficiently complete celebration. However, according to need, they may be integrated with a brief and suitable exegesis on the readings. Given the "contemplative" character of the themes, though, prolonged or distracting interventions ought to be avoided.

Where the opportunity presents itself, the outlines may even be used profitably as a Liturgy of the Word in Eucharistic Celebrations.

They might serve as a guide for Eucharistic adorations that are made weekly or monthly.

Finally, we believe that they can serve as a catechesis for the understanding of the Eucharistic mystery and of the fundamental, central, essential role of the Eucharist in the experience of faith.

This book was edited by Espedito D'Agostini, a Brother of the Servants of Mary at St. Egidio-Sotto il Monte, on the occasion of the Eucharistic Congress held in 1991 in Bergamo.

In the name of the community he developed and coordinated directions and texts, drawing from the brotherhood's thirty years of prayer experience. He did so with the hope of serving other communities also.

1

The Lord's Supper

The Lord's Supper is the center, the heart of the great mystery of the presence of Christ in every age.

And it is also the privileged means for penetrating this mystery and letting ourselves be enveloped by it, as by a zone that supports life.

If we remain on the surface or margin of this presence, this self-revelation of the Son of God; if we limit ourselves to a formal or ritual consummation of what the Lord's Supper offers; if we exhaust our contact with this immense reality in a sentimental experience; if the celebration of the Eucharist does not break down personal resistance, labeling and stereotyping; if it does not cause us to be open to an authentic interior and ecclesial experience of living together around Christ—then our faith does not identify us; it does not mature our personality according to the image of God which must reveal itself in us; it does not establish relationships of true universality, of mercy, tenderness, grace and reconciling selflessness.

Rather, hypocrisy divides and masks us: we don't have the right clothing.

Invitation to Prayer

v. The Lord will prepare for all his people
r. A banquet of rich food and pure wine.
v. What a table you have prepared for me!
r. My cup is overflowing!
v. Blessed are those invited to the wedding feast of the Lamb!
r. They will eat and be satisfied.

(Sing an appropriate opening hymn.)

Prayer

Holy Lord and Father,
to reveal your loving essence
and your perfect unity,
you gather us around the table of your Son,
who was given for our salvation.
Grant that we may eat and drink with dignity and without fear,
inebriating our minds and hearts with your infinite grace.
Through our Lord, Jesus Christ, your Son,
who is God and lives and reigns with you
in the unity of the Holy Spirit
forever and ever. Amen.

Reading

Then I heard what seemed to be the voice of a great multitude, like the sound of many waters and like the sound of mighty thunderpeals, crying, "Hallelujah! For the Lord our God the Almighty reigns. Let us rejoice and exult and give him the glory, for the marriage of the Lamb has come, and his Bride has made herself ready; it was granted her to be clothed with fine linen, bright and pure"—for the fine linen is the righteous deeds of the saints. And the angel said to me, "Write this: Blessed are those who are invited to the marriage supper of the Lamb." And he said to me, "These are true words of God" (Rev 19:6-9).

Psalm 23

The Lord is my shepherd, I shall not be in want.
He makes me lie down in green pastures,
he leads me beside quiet waters,
he restores my soul.
He guides me in paths of righteousness
for his name's sake.
Even though I walk
through the valley of the shadow of death,
I will fear no evil,
for you are with me;
your rod and staff,
they comfort me.
You prepare a table before me
in the presence of my enemies.
You anoint my head with oil;
my cup overflows.
Surely goodness and love will follow me
all the days of my life,
and I will dwell in the house of the Lord forever.

Thanks be to the Father, who from the dawning of the world
has blessed us in Christ, the only shepherd
who in the Spirit makes us walk in the heavens.

Gospel

On the first day of Unleavened Bread, when they sacrificed the passover lamb, his disciples said to him, "Where will you have us go and prepare for you to eat the passover?" And he sent two of his disciples, and said to them, "Go into the city, and a man carrying a jar of water will meet you; follow him, and wherever he enters, say to the householder, 'The Teacher says, Where is my guest room, where I am to eat the passover with my disciples?' And he will show you a large upper room furnished and ready; there prepare for us." And the disciples set out and went to the city, and found it as he had told them; and they prepared the passover....

And as they were eating, he took bread, and blessed, and broke it, and gave it to them, and said, "Take; this is my body." And he took a cup, and when he had given thanks he gave it to them, and they all drank of it. And he said to them, "This is my blood of the covenant, which is poured out for many. Truly, I say to you, I shall not drink again of the fruit of the vine until that day when I drink it new in the kingdom of God" (Mk 14:12-16, 22-26).

Meditation

Jesus was homeless, a displaced person, and he needed someone to give him a few things, at least for Passover.

There are certain days when one cannot eat by the side of the road or in the shade of a fig tree. Assailed by memories or overflowing with an infinite gift, the heart cannot express itself at just any crossroads. It craves a door that opens onto a large room; anything less would be sacrilegious.

This evening the love of Christ needs this room, large but not empty—as some of our cathedrals are. He needs to wash the feet of his poor apostles, to consecrate the Bread of life, to seal the institution with his testament.

And a nameless man, a householder, lends him his most beautiful room.

The homeless of every age, the dispossessed of today, who number in the millions, have their holy protector—a saint without a halo, without a church and without an altar—in him who lent Christ the first church and the first altar.

This man gave Christ the greatest thing he had, for around the great Sacrament everything should be great: room and heart, words and gestures.

Today, all churches should have the greatest spiritual breadth in order to welcome from every side the disinherited and distressed, to kiss the poor feet that have walked thousands of miles through mud or snow.

Thus was the first Eucharistic monstrance, prepared by that unknown householder.

I imagine him, with his wife and children, standing at the half-open door at the end of the banquet, a beggar more than a table companion of a Bread which he had prepared with his own hands and which the Christ had blessed and changed into the Bread of eternal life.[1]

Responsory

v. I have ardently desired to eat this Passover with you.
r. I have ardently desired to eat this Passover with you.
v. My time is near
r. To eat this Passover with you.
v. Glory to the Father, to the Son and to the Holy Spirit.
r. I have ardently desired to eat this Passover with you.

Intercessions

We implore the Father, who in his Son Jesus Christ gave us the food of immortality, and we say:

Satisfy our hunger, Lord.

Merciful Father, you have never abandoned your people in times of anguish and distress:
—as in the desert you sent manna to satisfy the hunger of the dying, so always help your Church with the food of eternal life.

Merciful Father, you did not forget Elijah in his desperation, but sent him an angel with the food that would sustain him to the mountain of your presence:
—give also to us the bread that strengthens, so we may continue to journey toward the Day of meeting you.

Merciful Father, you rewarded the faith of the widow of Zarephath with bread and oil until the end of the great famine:
—strengthen our weak faith, so we will not despair in time of trial.

Merciful Father, your Son Jesus multiplied bread for the hungry crowds, but in the desert he resisted the temptation to transform stones into bread:
—free us from the danger of making material interests a priority; help us to live only by your word.

Merciful Father, when the hour came for Jesus to die for us, he left his disciples a sign as a perpetual remembrance of him—the broken bread and the wine of the new covenant:
—grant that we who eat his body and drink his blood may also be for our brothers and sisters a bread that gives life and a chalice that radiates glory.

Prayer

O Father, giver of every good thing!
Give us bread for our physical strength,
give us the nourishment of your word
and of your doctrine.
Through Christ our Lord. Amen.
(Sing an appropriate closing hymn.)

Prayer to Mary

(optional)

A song blooms in my heart
as a gift to offer you, O Mother.
You persuaded your Son to accomplish
his first sign at the wedding of Cana.

You attentively said, "They have no more wine."
At that time your eye was the first to see
the joy of our banquets vanish,
but now, at this time, you know and can command.

Yes, we have no more wine, O Mother!
Our loves have no joy,
our fortune is without grace,
not even the feasts celebrate faith.

We give you glory, Father,
for Mary's faith in Christ's hour.
You satisfy us with that other wine of your Son—
the wine which is the Spirit, the wine that transforms us.

2

Do This in Memory of Me

To celebrate the "memorial" of the Lord is not simply to repeat and remember what he did one night.

Rather, it is to "do" what he did and continues to do, because we are aware of what he did with his own life "for us and for our salvation." He has given his body of flesh and poured out the cup of his blood for us and for all.

Therefore, to celebrate the Eucharist-memorial of the body and blood of Christ means that no other body may be mutilated, exploited or scorned on any assumption that this will promote the common good, nor that anyone's blood may be spilled in alliance or out of hostility. "This is my body which is for you," and this is the blood shed as an eternal covenant.

We receive this "memorial" as a new awareness of our entire being and our created existence within the divine-human event we have known in Christ Jesus. We must faithfully celebrate this with every fiber of our being until he comes and will be all in all.

Invitation to Prayer

v. This day will be for you a memorial;
r. You will celebrate it as a feast of the Lord.
v. From generation to generation
r. You will celebrate it as a perpetual rite.
v. The poor remember the Lord:
r. A new people will say: The Lord has done this!
(Sing an appropriate opening hymn.)

Prayer

Lord Jesus Christ,
who in the wonderful sacrament of the Eucharist
has left us a memorial of your passion,
grant that we may adore with living faith
the sacred mystery of your body and your blood,
in order to always experience within ourselves
the merits of your redemption.
You are God, and live and reign with the Father,
in the unity of the Holy Spirit
forever and ever. Amen.

Reading

For I received from the Lord what I also delivered to you, that the Lord Jesus on the night when he was betrayed took bread, and when he had given thanks, he broke it, and said, "This is my body which is for you. Do this in remembrance of me." In the same way also the cup, after supper, saying, "This cup is the new covenant in my blood. Do this, as often as you drink it, in remembrance of me." For as often as you eat this bread and drink the cup, you proclaim the Lord's death until he comes (1 Cor 11:23-26).

Psalm 103:1-8

Praise the Lord, O my soul;
all my inmost being, praise his holy name.
Praise the Lord, O my soul,
and forget not all his benefits—
who forgives all your sins,
and heals all your diseases,
who redeems your life from the pit
and crowns you with love and compassion,
who satisfies your desires with good things
so that your youth is renewed like the eagle's.
The Lord works righteousness
and justice for all the oppressed.
He made known his ways to Moses,
his deeds to the people of Israel:
The Lord is compassionate and gracious,
slow to anger, abounding in love.

Glory to the Father, to the Son and to the Holy Spirit
for the love, faith and hope
which have made us sharers in the divinity.

Gospel

When the hour came, he sat at table, and the apostles with him. And he said to them, "I have earnestly desired to eat this passover with you before I suffer; for I tell you I shall not eat it until it is fulfilled in the kingdom of God." And he took a cup, and when he had given thanks he said, "Take this, and divide it among yourselves; for I tell you that from now on I shall not drink of the fruit of the vine until the kingdom of God comes." And he took bread, and when he had given thanks he broke it and gave it to them, saying, "This is my body which is given for you. Do this in remembrance of me." And likewise the cup after supper, saying, "This cup which is poured out for you is the new covenant in my blood" (Lk 22:14-20).

Meditation

In ancient times, a pillar of stone was considered a polarizer of generative power. References to this connection are frequent in the Old Testament: "You were unmindful of the Rock that begot you" (Dt 32:18); "The Lord is my rock" (Ps 18:2; 92:15; 95:1). In "memorial," Joshua set up the twelve stones, indicating the generative power of the twelve tribes of Israel. We should not be disturbed by this realistic image, strange to our mentality. In the Old Testament God is experienced as the one who makes fruitful. This is not a rare notion and perhaps it is fundamental. It is enough to read Chapter 30 of Genesis to realize this. I will limit myself to citing verse 22, which may be translated thus: "God also remembered Rachel, God heard her and made her fruitful, she conceived and bore a son."

The words: "Do this in memory of me," do not mean to repeat an act in remembrance of Christ's love, but to complete an action which physically transforms the bread and wine by the saving power of Christ. Through the work of the sacramental words, the bread and wine become the carrier of Christ's presence in the midst of humankind. The fruitful and transmuting presence of the rock which is the human heart [of Christ] in the bread and wine are the essence and life-giving song of all creation, the sign of the ultimate reality of God.[2]

Do This in Memory of Me

Responsory

v. I will recount the marvels of the Lord;
   I will remember that you alone are just.
*r. I will recount the marvels of the Lord;
   I will remember that you alone are just.*
v. I will sing for ever of your love.
r. I will remember that you alone are just.
v. Glory to the Father, to the Son and to the Holy Spirit.
*r. I will recount the marvels of the Lord;
   I will remember that you alone are just.*

Intercessions

We pray to you, Lord Jesus Christ, the bread of life come down from heaven to fill to the brim our hunger for immortality. We say:

You are our life, Lord.

O Christ, son of the living God, you left us the Eucharistic bread and wine as signs of your presence in our midst:
—grant that your Church may always be reinvigorated by the celebration of your mysteries.

O Christ, you are the head of the body, the principle of unity of all believers:
—grant that there may no longer exist divisions among those who eat the one bread of life.

O Christ, you are in us as the seed of immortality, the certainty that we will also rise with you in glory:
—help us not to despair when we bitterly feel the distance that separates us from the fullness of the Kingdom.

O Christ, you have commanded us to offer again in time the memorial of your death and resurrection until the day of your return:
—grant that we may not become tired of waiting for you, and that we may proclaim to the world that you have conquered death forever.

O Christ, you are the presence of joy in our Eucharistic assembly, you are the friend who gives strength and hope:
—be always in our midst, so that we may have a place with you at the banquet in the last times.

Prayer

We thank you, Lord Jesus,
for having shown us
that we cannot know you through discussions,
for pointing out the silent gesture
of the breaking of the bread
as a sign that reveals you.
We ask you for dynamism of soul
to express your presence always
with the breaking of your bread and ours.
You are God and you live and reign
forever and ever. Amen.

(Sing an appropriate closing hymn.)

Prayer to Mary

(optional)

The mother said to the servants:
"Do whatever he tells you."
They are your last words, Mary.
We never hear your voice again;

Now the son will begin to speak.
Listen to what he says!
It is heaven, it is God who speaks, O people,
Do only what he says!

Thus the miracle is still accomplished.
The Father's voice still resounds
as at Christ's baptism in the Jordan:
"He is my beloved Son: listen to him!"

Most holy and beloved Trinity!
With all creation we sing
of Mary's faith, of Mary's silence:
we sing of the abundance of wine.

3

The Bread of Life

*L*ook at the "bread" that is placed on the table. Do not let it scandalize you that, after he chose to become human like you and to meet such a difficult death, now the Son of God has decided to be present in the form of bread—he whom not even the heavens can contain.

He—the life of every life, the love of all loves, the heart of all creation—is bread that you can eat. And so, eat infinite life, nourish yourself on immense love, take within yourself, within your body, the eternal impulse that moves all creation and holds it together. At the breaking of the bread, the eyes of your mind and heart open. You feel the burning ardor of fire within you, incorruptible energy that gives to your being the savor and scent and radiant joy of the bread you eat.

Invitation to Prayer

v. The Lord made manna rain down for their food:
r. He gave them bread from heaven.
v. Human beings ate the bread of angels!
r. Oh, the abundance of food that he gave!
v. I am the true bread which comes down from heaven:
r. And he gave life to the world.
(Sing an appropriate opening hymn.)

Prayer

Your bread, Father, nourishes our flesh
and fills our souls to overflowing;
sustain our efforts and enlighten our minds.
Nourished by you,
we are sustained in this passing world,
that we may reach your kingdom,
where everything is permanent.
Through our Lord Jesus Christ, your Son, who is God
and lives and reigns with you in the unity of the Holy Spirit
forever and ever. Amen.

Reading

Do you not know that a little leaven leavens the whole lump? Cleanse out the old leaven that you may be a new lump, as you really are unleavened. For Christ, our paschal lamb, has been sacrificed. Let us, therefore, celebrate the festival, not with the old leaven, the leaven of malice and evil, but with the unleavened bread of sincerity and truth (1 Cor 5:6b-8).

Psalm 147:12-20

Extol the Lord, O Jerusalem;
praise your God, O Zion,
for he strengthens the bars of your gates
and blesses your people within you.
He grants peace to your borders
and satisfies you with the finest of wheat.
He sends his command to the earth;
his word runs swiftly.
He spreads the snow like wool
and scatters the frost like ashes.
He hurls down his hail like pebbles.
Who can withstand with his icy blast?
He sends his word and melts them;
he stirs up his breezes, and the waters flow.
He has revealed his word to Jacob,
his laws and decrees to Israel.
He has done this for no other nation;
they do not know his laws.
Praise the Lord.

Christ, splendor of divine light,
all creation reveals and exalts you.

Gospel

So they said to him, "Then what sign do you do, that we may see, and believe you? What work do you perform? Our fathers ate the manna in the wilderness; as it is written, 'He gave them bread from heaven to eat.'" Jesus then said to them, "Truly, truly, I say to you, it was not Moses who gave you the bread from heaven; my

Father gives you the true bread from heaven. For the bread of God is that which comes down from heaven, and gives life to the world." They said to him, "Lord, give us this bread always."

Jesus said to them, "I am the bread of life; he who comes to me shall not hunger, and he who believes in me shall never thirst" (Jn 6:30-36).

Meditation

This general understanding of nourishment gives us a surer grasp of Christian teaching.

Christ tells us that whoever eats his flesh will have eternal life. That is, whoever consumes Christ in his totality, as the Word who became flesh, achieves true life. In Christ, flesh and word are one and the same thing. To eat Christ's flesh is to eat his word. This act confers true and eternal life. With the injunction to eat his flesh, Christ has expressed one of the most profound analogies of nature. The process of assimilation of his word is parallel to that of physical assimilation.

To eat the flesh-word of Christ means to decompose it into its basic elements, to extract what best corresponds to our personality and to find an original way of applying it to ourselves. As with every species of animal, so every individual person assimilates the amino acids that they most need.

Therefore, we must utilize these elements for the reconstruction of a personality that conforms to our individual nature, different from that of every other human being, in the same way that the protein molecules we reconstruct from the common amino-acids are different from those of any other living being.

The conclusion is that there is no uniformity in the assimilation of the flesh-word; no equal expression of living the reality of

Christ; no repetitive monotony in the queue of the faithful who truly want to put on Christ.

From the outset, this is a rejection of every educational system that forms individuals to be too much alike, to the detriment of each one's specific characteristics. It is disapproval of all uniformity, of arbitrary commands, of merely passive obedience, of everything that tends to produce a monochord, to level individuals. Each of the faithful is called to live the flesh-word of Christ in a personal way, analogous to the digestion and assimilation of food. On the basis of this new insight, we accent the phenomenon of spiritual digestion. In the double movement of analysis and synthesis, Jesus Christ has united himself to the unique personality of each individual, which is a reality different from all others. Each person builds up his or her protein molecules differently than any other living being.[3]

Responsory

v. Behold the bread of angels, bread of pilgrims,
true bread of children.
r. *Behold the bread of angels, bread of pilgrims,*
true bread of children.
v. Living bread which gives life:
r. *True bread of children.*
v. Glory to the Father, to the Son and to the Holy Spirit.
r. *Behold the bread of angels, bread of pilgrims,*
true bread of children.

Intercessions

We lift up our needs to the Lord Jesus. He is the inexhaustible fountainhead of life which truly sustains every person, so we say:

Give us your bread of life, Lord.

Lord, give us your living water, so that we may not die of thirst:
—give us your bread, so that our souls may not die of hunger.

To do your will is also our food and drink:
—accomplish your work, Lord.

Lord, may each one of us be a true adorer of the Father:
—in spirit and truth.

Lord, may your Church be a new and free people:
—the dwelling of your Holy Spirit.

May all humanity, beyond every division and culture:
—become your temple, Lord.

May everyone become the body of your Church in the one faith:
—in the one hope of salvation, in the one love which you are, Lord.

May no one despise or doubt another:
—so that no people or continent may consider other peoples or continents lost.

May all acknowledge you as the only and true Messiah, O Jesus:
—so that all will invite you to dwell in their land.

Prayer

May the bread which we prepare on the table, O Lord,
help us to live and radiate your love.
It can feed the hungry, heal the sick,
give birth to peace and trust, dispel anguish
and prosper the vision of true joy,
which is in you and is never consumed.
Through Christ our Lord. Amen.

(Sing an appropriate closing hymn.)

Prayer to Mary

(optional)

Your first word, Mary,
we ask you to receive into your heart,
as if it were still possible
to conceive God's Word for us.

"Never ask for signs or reasons—
only believe and love.
His Spirit descends on all of you,
and you will be his own flesh."

You are blessed because you believed,
and thus he could pour out upon you
the living word of the Father,
O blessed dwelling of God.

To you Father, Son and Spirit
be thanks and glory for giving
the entire world this mother,
hope of all the living.

4

The Blood of the New and Perfect Covenant

A small cup of wine stands next to the bread on the altar for the Eucharist. The eyes of faith must enlarge that cup to immense dimensions, so that it will contain all creatures in a new, perfect and eternal covenant.

The believer must experience being immersed in this living liquid, as in a vast womb which welcomes the infinite divine seeds, nourishes them and brings them to maturity.

Every person, every creature is a pearl of blood in this chalice, gathered from the fountain flowing from the pierced side of Christ. Every creature is a single grape taken from the one vine to produce the new wine that gives the joyous inebriation of hope and the strength of truth, until it bursts the old wineskins of so much slavery and self interest.

Invitation to Prayer

v. The Lamb has been slain:
r. With his blood he has redeemed
v. People of every tribe, language, race and nation;
r. And he has made them priests of the only God.
v. This is the blood of the eternal covenant:
r. In his bath all are cleansed.

(Sing an appropriate opening hymn.)

Prayer

Lord God, the new and perfect covenant
which you have established in the blood of your Son
unites us inseparably to you.
In our veins,
in our every inmost fiber,
grant that we may feel flowing
the inexhaustible fountain of life.
Through our Lord Jesus Christ, your Son, who is God
and lives and reigns with you in the unity of the Holy Spirit
forever and ever. Amen.

Reading

For if the sprinkling of defiled persons with the blood of goats and bulls and with the ashes of a heifer sanctifies for the purification of the flesh, how much more shall the blood of Christ, who through the eternal Spirit offered himself without blemish to God, purify your conscience from dead works to serve the living God.

Therefore he is the mediator of a new covenant, so that those who are called may receive the promised eternal inheritance, since a death has occurred which redeems them from the transgressions under the first covenant. For where a will is involved, the death of the one who made it must be established. For a will takes effect only at death, since it is not in force as long as the one who made it is alive. Hence even the first covenant was not ratified without blood. For when every commandment of the law had been declared by Moses to all the people, he took the blood of calves and goats, with water and scarlet wool and hyssop, and sprinkled both the book itself and all the people, saying, "This is the blood of the covenant which God commanded you." And in the same way he sprinkled with the blood both the tent and all the vessels used in worship. Indeed, under the law almost everything is purified with blood, and without the shedding of blood there is no forgiveness of sins (Heb 9:13-22).

Psalm 16

Keep me safe, O God,
for in you I take refuge.
I said to the Lord, "You are my Lord;
apart from you I have no good thing."
As for the saints who are in the land,
they are the glorious ones in whom is all my delight.
The sorrows of those will increase
who run after other gods.
I will not pour out their libations of blood
or take up their names on my lips.
Lord, you have assigned me my portion and my cup;
you have made my lot secure.
The boundary lines have fallen for me in pleasant places;

surely I have a delightful inheritance.
I will praise the Lord, who counsels me;
even at night my heart instructs me.
I have set the Lord always before me.
Because he is at my right hand,
I will not be shaken.
Therefore my heart is glad and my tongue rejoices;
my body also will rest secure,
because you will not abandon me to the grave,
nor will you let your Holy One see decay.
You have made known to me the path of life;
you will fill me with joy in your presence,
with eternal pleasures at your right hand.

To you, Father, God of life,
who raised your Son from the dead,
we sing in the Holy Spirit,
joyful that we will live forever.

Gospel

Since it was the day of Preparation, in order to prevent the bodies from remaining on the cross on the sabbath (for that sabbath was a high day), the Jews asked Pilate that their legs might be broken, and that they might be taken away. So the soldiers came and broke the legs of the first, and of the other who had been crucified with him; but when they came to Jesus and saw that he was already dead, they did not break his legs. But one of the soldiers pierced his side with a spear, and at once there came out blood and water (Jn 19:31-34).

Meditation

The scandal and folly of which Paul speaks (cf. 1 Cor 1:18-25) can seem strange! But it is precisely the cross, signifying the greatest distance from God, which affirms his nearness to us in our most hidden depths and reveals him with infinite love. On the cross, apex of desperation and sin, of chaos and lack of potential, of evil and destruction, God unites himself with the extremes of creation. Although in the act of creation he separated the object of his love from himself, in the passion he embraces that object again—just as it is—and fills it with his presence. The very negation of God on the cross is God, Love itself. The power of his hands has created us, placing us outside him. The impotence of his love has saved us, bringing him to us. Because of this, the Fathers understood the cross as the place where the search of God and of humanity is consummated, as the nuptial bed that finally unites the two in one love. "Kiss me with the kisses of your mouth" (Song 1:2) is the great unconfessed desire, the void within the human person. God has placed it in our hearts, making us in his image and likeness. It is an absolute thirst that no water can quench, an inextinguishable fire that no ashes of death can smother. Upon the cross of Jesus the breath of God and man finally become only one pant of love, of death and of life. Calvary is the place of this kiss on the lips, where human breath enters into God and the spirit of God enters into humankind.

The crucified humanity of Jesus is a manifestation of God, inasmuch as God is distant and yet burdened with love. But this is also the martyrdom of a man who responds "yes" to this love and unites himself to God. The cursed flesh of the innocent one who hangs from the wood unites God and humanity. This torn humanity reveals the divinity as love. "Mercy and truth have met, justice and peace have kissed," as Psalm 85 prophesies (cf. v. 10). The cross is the place where mercy and truth meet: the mercy of God and the truth of humanity. Thus the justice of God becomes our peace.[4]

Responsory

v. You have redeemed us, Lord,
   with your blood that was shed.
*r. You have redeemed us, Lord,
   with your blood that was shed.*
v. You have reconciled humanity with God,
r. With your blood that was shed.
v. Glory to the Father, to the Son, and to the Holy Spirit.
*r. You have redeemed us, Lord,
   with your blood that was shed.*

Intercessions

Uniting ourselves to the Spirit who prays within us, we present our petitions to God and say:

Draw us to yourself, Lord.

God of love, you have established an eternal covenant with your people, a covenant ratified in the blood shed by your Son:
—help us to be faithful to your will, so that we may be in the midst of the world a sign that you never abandon humanity.

God of love, we have known you in Jesus Christ, but we are often doubtful and risk yielding to the temptation to substitute empty idols for you:
—remind us that you are the fountain of life and that all beings have in you a destiny of infinite greatness.

The Blood of the New and Perfect Covenant

God of love, at times we tire of seeking you, because it seems that the more we believe you are near, the more you distance yourself:
—increase our faith with the gift of your Spirit, the only certainty that even now opens the horizons of your kingdom for us.

God of love, the time in which we live is evil and we do not see signs of your day, when all creatures will be clothed in your splendor:
—enlighten our eyes, so that we may discern the signs of your coming into our midst.

God of love, you have always sent prophets to your people, so that hope will not be quenched:
—guard our frailty and send us again someone to show us the paths on which we will meet you.

Prayer

Father, make us truly your children,
aware of the eternal source
that gives life to each of us,
in the certainty that in you there is no end,
but eternal continuation.
Through Christ our Lord. Amen.

(Sing an appropriate closing hymn.)

Prayer to Mary

(optional)

You went to a marriage feast—
with your Son to a wedding, O Mother,

but he dreamed of another meal
and already saw the mountain of sorrows.

Here he shows forth his glory,
and his disciples believe in him:
but can they fathom that glory's real meaning
and what "hour" it is that must come?

And yet you need to sing, O Mother:
all foreshadows another alliance.
Today you have revealed the Lamb;
no more shall we lack his wine.

Glory to the Father, whose new love
he gives us from then and forever—
love which only the Son reveals
and the Spirit gives to every true lover.

5

Eucharist: Revelation of Love

*B*y *coming to us under the appearances of bread and wine, Christ Jesus has placed into our fragile hands everything that he is. He has made his presence perceptible to our senses.*

Not only does his love reveal itself in his total gift of himself, of his humanity and divinity (as forgiveness, liberation, mercy, communion, fraternity); it is also revealed in the way he makes himself known: passively, as a "place" to which we can choose to have access with the limitations of our awareness and the diversity of our existence, and as an object to be enjoyed by the senses through the action of eating and drinking.

If you know what you are eating and drinking—as, out of love for yourself and your health, you must do with any food—if you know what your hands grasp and raise to your lips, you flood your being with a loving revelation that regenerates you. Your mind, heart and spirit are filled by a unifying will. God, other human beings, animate and inanimate things, time, places, everything, distinct and united, live within you in a fascinating harmony, which you will not venture to sunder.

Invitation to Prayer

v. We wait for you, O Lord:
r. You shower your love upon us.
v. How precious, O God, is your love:
r. Your wings extend over all creation.
v. Love is sweeter than life:
r. Sweetest, O God, is your love.

(Sing an appropriate opening hymn.)

Prayer

Father,
Love, spring of living water, we call upon you!
We need your light,
your zest, your freshness.
Melt what is frozen, warm what is tepid,
enlighten what is dark, water what is dry.
Through our Lord Jesus Christ, your Son, who is God
and lives and reigns with you in the unity of the Holy Spirit
forever and ever. Amen.

Reading

Whoever confesses that Jesus is the Son of God, God abides in him, and he in God. So we know and believe the love God has for us. God is love, and he who abides in love abides in God, and God abides in him. In this is love perfected with us, that we may have confidence for the day of judgment, because as he is so are we in this world. There is no fear in love, but perfect love casts out fear. For fear has to do with punishment, and he who fears is not perfected in love. We love, because he first loved us. If anyone says, "I love God," and hates his brother, he is a liar; for he who does not love his brother whom he has seen, cannot love God whom he has not seen. And this commandment we have from him, that he who loves God should love his brother also (1 Jn 4:15-21).

Psalm 85

You showed favor to your land, O Lord;
You restored the fortunes of Jacob.
You forgave the iniquity of your people
and covered all their sins.
You set aside all your wrath
and turned from your fierce anger.
Restore us again, O God our Savior,
and put away your displeasure toward us.
Will you be angry with us forever?
Will you prolong your anger through all generations?
Will you not revive us again,
that your people may rejoice in you?
Show us your unfailing love, O Lord,
and grant us your salvation.
I will listen to what God the Lord will say;
he promises peace to his people, his saints—
but let them not return to folly.
Surely his salvation is near those who fear him,
that his glory may dwell in our land.
Love and faithfulness meet together;
righteousness and peace kiss each other.
Faithfulness springs forth from the earth,
and righteousness looks down from heaven.
The Lord will indeed give what is good,

and our land will yield its harvest.
Righteousness goes before him
and prepares the way for his steps.

Together with all creation,
which groans in the hope of being free,
we sing always to the living Christ,
to him who comes to save us from death.

Gospel

"I do not pray for these only, but also for those who believe in me through their word, that they may all be one; even as you, Father, are in me, and I in you, that they also may be in us, so that the world may believe that you have sent me. The glory which you have given me I have given them, that they may be one even as we are one, I in them and you in me, that they may become perfectly one, so that the world may know that you have sent me and have loved them even as you have loved me. Father, I desire that they also, whom you have given me, may be with me where I am, to behold my glory which you have given me in your love for me before the foundation of the world. O righteous Father, the world has not known you, but I have known you; and these know that you have sent me. I made known to them your name, and I will make it known, that the love with which you have loved me may be in them, and I in them" (Jn 17:20-26).

Meditation

"This is my body for you"—"This is my blood for you"—"Do this in memory of me"—"Take and eat." In the heart of the great Eucharistic prayer, the Father through the power of the Spirit accomplishes the words of Jesus and makes them current. That bread and that wine really and truly change into the presence of the Risen Lord, the Living One. The Lord presents himself to his followers as a voice that recalls and as food that communicates.

The Risen One present in our midst reminds us that his "birth" is dictated by *agape*. Agape directs his "today" as an existence that has become bread, water, light, life, word to the hungry, to the thirsty, to the blind, to the dead, to the exiled. Agape is the hidden reality that led him to his "hour," to death, to a death accepted and lived as a pure gift for the multitude, as remission for the sin of the world.

The Risen One entered death and changed its significance. From a negative event, dark and destructive and against nature, Jesus transformed it into the reason for his birth and life: to live for humanity to the last drop of his blood. Thus, death becomes the supreme gesture of love, the moment in which the gift of self reaches its fullness. It is a gift for humanity that Jesus lived in obedience to *agape*, whose name is God. This offering is free: "I lay down my life, that I may take it up again. No one takes it from me, but I lay it down of my own accord" (Jn 10:17-18).

This offering is suffered: "'My soul is very sorrowful, even to death.'... And going a little farther, he fell on the ground and prayed that, if it were possible, the hour might pass from him. And he said, 'Abba, Father, all things are possible to you; remove this cup from me; yet not what I will, but what you will'" (Mk 14:34-36). This offering is loving: "Greater love has no man than this, that a man lay down his life for his friends" (Jn 15:13).

And so the Living One reminds us that the body broken and the blood poured out are the fruit of a free and painful obedience to Love out of love for each human being, whom God calls "friend."[5]

Responsory

v. The love of God has appeared
bringing salvation for all.
*r. The love of God has appeared
bringing salvation for all.*
v. May the Father's love be with us,
and the unity of the Spirit
r. Bringing salvation for all.
v. Glory to the Father, to the Son and to the Holy Spirit.
*r. The love of God has appeared
bringing salvation for all.*

Intercessions

To God who is love; to the Son who reveals this; to the Spirit who pours love into our hearts, we direct our prayer. And we say:

In you, Lord, love is perfect.

Love, who formed me in your faceless image, Love who tenderly recreated me after the fall:

—Love, I surrender. I will be your eternal splendor.

Love, who chose me from the day you molded my body, Love, hidden in human flesh, now completely like me:

—Love, I surrender. I will be your eternal possession.

Love, who at your pleasure fashioned my soul, my senses, my whole being, Love, who envelops me in your abyss, my heart can resist no longer:

—I surrender, Love, my eternal life.

Prayer

O Father, love has its source in you,
and in you it will have its end.
Father, teach us to love!
For too long Love has not been loved.
Father, teach us to love,
because only love will restore in us
what has been squandered;
only love will liberate in us
what is enchained;
only love will resurrect in us
what is has died.
We ask this through Christ, our Lord. Amen.
(Sing an appropriate closing hymn.)

Prayer to Mary

(optional)

May all lips be purified;
May piety and beauty inspire a song:
May psalms still rise up to Zion,
proclaiming: "See, your king comes."

Let us again sing with the prophet:
"Rejoice, daughter of Zion, beloved one—
now your God, the Lord, is with you:
blessed are you because you have believed!"

The Virgin Mother leads the procession—
she, the first true city of love:
she is the true type of Zion,
and the divine dawn of new times.

Your king, your meek Lord, declares:
"I will make to dwell in your midst
a humble and poor people"—a sign
that the Lord will never leave or betray us.

Open your gates, O Jerusalem,
he is the king you have always awaited;
exult, old and new Israel:
the whole world now follows him.

6

Eucharist: Mystery of Communion

If we did not have the opportunity for everyone to eat of the one bread and drink of the one cup, we would not be able to understand what communion is. Instead, because we receive life and nourishment from a single source, we understand the mystery of communion that we have within and among us. The same God who is "in our midst," is the captivating magnetic pole of all creation. He is the inspiration and reason for our every emotion and our every thought—which must, however, meekly encounter all other emotions and thoughts. Every good proceeds from him and only from him, so he is truly Lord of all.

Certainly you have your life, your body, your possessions.... But you are Christ's and Christ is God's. This is the communion we experience when our lips draw near to the one cup, filled with the redeeming and liberating blood; when we place in our mouth the body that has been given for "us" and that gathers within our members the signs of a mysterious and efficacious reality.

Invitation to Prayer

v. Blessed are those who make you their refuge,
r. Pilgrims who carry your ways in their heart.
v. As the mountains surround Jerusalem,
r. So the Lord surrounds his people.
v. When I shall be lifted up from the earth
r. I will draw all to myself.

(Sing an appropriate opening hymn.)

Prayer

O Lord, our ever more intense communion
with the mystery of your presence
makes us grow and mature
in the harmony that is yours;
Grant that all of us, as one, sole reality,
may stretch out our hands to you
to be flooded by your light
and manifest you in the world.
Through our Lord Jesus Christ, your Son, who is God
and lives and reigns with you in the unity of the Holy Spirit
forever and ever. Amen.

Reading

And they devoted themselves to the apostles' teaching and fellowship, to the breaking of bread and the prayers.

And fear came upon every soul; and many wonders and signs were done through the apostles. And all who believed were together and had all things in common; and they sold their possessions and goods and distributed them to all, as any had need. And day by day, attending the temple together and breaking bread in their homes, they partook of food with glad and generous hearts, praising God and having favor with all the people. And the Lord added to their number day by day those who were being saved (Acts 2:42-47).

Psalm 128

Blessed are all who fear the Lord,
who walk in his ways.
You will eat the fruit of your labor;
blessings and prosperity will be yours.
Your wife will be like a fruitful vine
within your house;
your sons will be like olive shoots
around your table.
Thus is the man blessed
who fears the Lord.
May the Lord bless you from Zion
all the days of your life;
may you see the prosperity of Jerusalem,
and may you live to see your children's children.
Peace be upon Israel.

Glory to the Father, to the Son, and to the Holy Spirit,
as it was in the beginning, is now and will be forever. Amen.

Gospel

"I am the true vine, and my Father is the vinedresser. Every branch of mine that bears no fruit, he takes away, and every branch that does bear fruit he prunes, that it may bear more fruit. You are already made clean by the word which I have spoken to you. Abide in me, and I in you. As the branch cannot bear fruit by itself, unless it abides in the vine, neither can you, unless you abide in me. I am the vine, you are the branches. He who abides in me, and I in him, he it is that bears much fruit, for apart from me you can do nothing. If a man does not abide in me, he is cast forth as a branch and withers; and the branches are gathered, thrown into the fire and burned. If you abide in me, and my words abide in you, ask whatever you will, and it shall be done for you. By this my Father is glorified, that you bear much fruit, and so prove to be my disciples. As the Father has loved me, so have I loved you; abide in my love. If you keep my commandments, you will abide in my love, just as I have kept my Father's commandments and abide in his love. These things I have spoken to you, that my joy may be in you, and that your joy may be full" (Jn 15:1-11).

Meditation

Since Christ's entire life in present in the Eucharist, the whole plan of God is here. Here the purpose of creation and of the incarnation is accomplished. Here the Church begins, the community that is a type of the kingdom to come.

For one who believes, I repeat, the Eucharist is the ultimate goal of world history. It is not by chance that the Eucharist is consumed as a meal, as a marriage feast. Either: "Everyone come to the wedding," or: "of all those invited (who did not respond to the invitation), not one will enjoy my supper" (cf. Lk 14:15-24). All those who do not form the body—who do not live by love—will not have a place in the kingdom. The Eucharist judges us individually and judges the Church herself—to see whether the Church is a real community, a real type of the kingdom.

The Eucharist is the "all" that "has been accomplished"—both in the self-giving of God and in the self-giving of humanity. God makes himself food and we have eaten; thus, everyone can say: "I live, not I, but the Lord lives in me." Yes, it is God who is eaten, who disappears within the human person. In this self-giving love, behold the source of the world's unity—the overcoming of all selfishness, the removal of every barrier. The Father's work culminates in the Eucharist. From the beginning he wanted a covenant with all humanity: that finally the kingdom of God might be realized! The Son's work culminates in the Eucharist, for this is the last act of the Christ of God. "Take and eat me, for I want to be within you forever, so that you may already live of me who have conquered death and therefore may have everlasting life within you." In fact, to live the Eucharist in all its fullness—if one succeeds in doing so—is already to be in the kingdom. A saint used to pray: "Lord, on that day when I make a true, perfect Communion, with complete understanding and commitment, take me with you, because I will already be in your kingdom." But when can anyone claim to have made a perfect Communion?

The ultimate goal of the Holy Spirit's action is to achieve this Eucharist—that is, a complete community, a true Church, the kingdom fulfilled. Even more, the purpose of the Spirit's action is to achieve cosmic communion, the objective of all creation. Everything tends towards unity. Humanity is one; the body is one. It can never be sufficiently repeated that history's goal is the union of the entire human race in love; the joining of all creatures in peace; the fulfillment of "the groaning of creation."[6]

Responsory

v. God fulfills his plan
   to unite all things in Christ.
*r. God fulfills his plan
   to unite all things in Christ.*
v. He has made known to us his loving will:
r. To unite all things in Christ.
v. Glory to the Father, to the Son and to the Holy Spirit.
*r. God fulfills his plan
   to unite all things in Christ.*

Intercessions

We raise our prayer to Christ, in whom we have received the very life of God the Father and the love of the Holy Spirit, and we ask:

Conform us to yourself, O Christ.

O true vine, grant that we may always be your branches and bear fruit in you:
—pruned by the vinedresser, may we bear even more fruit.

O living bread, be our nourishment:
—and make us food of life for our brothers and sisters.

O master, you know everything:
—teach us the one thing necessary.

O good shepherd, you know your sheep:
—grant that we may know you, listen to your voice and follow you.

O way, truth and life, welcome us travelers:
—seekers, who want to live forever.

O light of the world, conquer the darkness:
—O Son of God, make us know the Father.

O Son of man, you have borne the burdens of all:
—teach us to help and serve others and to give our lives for them.

Prayer

O Father,
through communion with you
and with all beings,
dissolve every illusion,
free the universe from its painful obsession,
end its nightmare,
reawaken everyone to the knowledge
of your unique Reality.
Through Christ our Lord. Amen.

(Sing an appropriate closing hymn.)

Prayer to Mary

(optional)

We sing thanks to you, O Mother!
A sigh escapes from your heart:
"Son, why have you done this to us?
Your father and I have sought you sorrowing!"

"Did you not know that I must be concerned
with my Father's business?"
Not even you know, Mother,
but you will know it tomorrow, and every day,

when he will say that his food and drink
is only to do the will of the Father,
and that his mother and brothers and sisters
are those who listen to the Father and love him.

Glory be to God, because in his Son
a greater family exists,
where no one feels alone any longer,
and in the Spirit all sing to Love.

7

Eucharist: Language of the Inexpressible

No one can say, "God," unless empowered by the Spirit. It is the Spirit who cries out from every welcoming heart with indescribable words in a language impossible for the human mind to comprehend. The inexpressible language by which humans and God meet one another in a wonderful unity is the eternal, life-giving Word. Marvelous things have happened through this Word, but you will do even greater ones!

What we cannot hear with our ears and our lips cannot pronounce; what our mind cannot contain and our spirit cannot experience; what can fully enlighten us and bring our plans to perfection, making each of us the splendid and faithful image of the God-who-has-no-name—this is the Word made flesh and blood, substantial food for the revelation and gift of the one true life.

Invitation to Prayer

v. Who can tell the wonders of the Lord,
r. And make all his praise resound?
v. Terrible and holy is his name.
r. The beginning of wisdom is the fear of the Lord.
v. Who will measure the power of the Lord?
r. Who can recount his mercies?

(Sing an appropriate opening hymn.)

Prayer

Eternal Father,
we are gathered here together to call upon you,
aware that words can only hinder
the thrust of our souls toward you.
You are good, you are master, you are wise.
You who are the life, you who are the truth,
accept our imperfect way of understanding you,
our imperfect way of being with you.
Through our Lord Jesus Christ, your Son, who is God
and lives and reigns with you in the unity of the Holy Spirit
forever and ever. Amen.

Reading

To me, though I am the very least of all the saints, this grace was given, to preach to the Gentiles the unsearchable riches of Christ, and to make all men see what is the plan of the mystery hidden for ages in God who created all things; that through the church the manifold wisdom of God might now be made known to the principalities and powers in the heavenly places. This was according to the eternal purpose which he has realized in Christ Jesus our Lord, in whom we have boldness and confidence of access through our faith in him (Eph 3:8-12).

Psalm 19

The heavens declare the glory of God;
the skies proclaim the work of his hands.
Day after day they pour forth speech;
night after night they display knowledge.
There is no speech or language
where their voice is not heard.
Their voice goes out into all the earth,
their words to the ends of the world.
In the heavens he has pitched a tent for the sun,
which is like a bridegroom coming forth from his pavilion,
like a champion rejoicing to run his course.
It rises at one end of the heavens
and makes its circuit to the other;
nothing is hidden from its heat.
The law of the Lord is perfect,
reviving the soul.
The statutes of the Lord are trustworthy,
making wise the simple;
The precepts of the Lord are right,
giving joy to the heart.
The commands of the Lord are radiant,
giving light to the eyes.
The fear of the Lord is pure,
enduring forever;
the ordinances of the Lord are sure

and altogether righteous.
They are more precious than gold,
than much pure gold;
they are sweeter than honey,
than honey from the comb.
By them is your servant warned;
in keeping them there is great reward.
Who can discern his errors?
Forgive my hidden faults.
Keep your servant also from willful sins;
may they not rule over me.
Then will I be blameless,
innocent of great transgression.
May the words of my mouth and the meditation of my heart
be pleasing in your sight,
O Lord, my Rock and my Redeemer.

Glory to the Father in the highest heavens,
glory to the Son, his eternal splendor,
glory to the Spirit, heart of the world:
and also to humanity, his image, be glory!

Gospel

"I have yet many things to say to you, but you cannot bear them now. When the Spirit of truth comes, he will guide you into all the truth; for he will not speak on his own authority, but whatever he hears he will speak, and he will declare to you the things that are to come. He will glorify me, for he will take what is mine and declare it to you. All that the Father has is mine; therefore I said that he will take what is mine and declare it to you" (Jn 16:12-15).

Meditation

Despite the uprooting of us moderns from nature, our essential fabric remains unchanged: birth, infancy, adolescence, maturity, death. Also unchanging are the substances that constitute part of life: seed, blood, bread, food, water, oil, wine, salt, wood, rock, metal. These substances have been used in various ways in religious rites, while preserving their full validity in daily life.

Before they take on a religious significance and value, sacred signs belong to reality. Knowledge transforms them, pointing out aspects of them that are imperceptible to the senses. Although salt is the same whether it is used on food or in a rite, in the rite it expresses something more of what it is, something that goes unnoticed in daily life.

Sacred signs have a biological basis that should never be forgotten. Perhaps the impoverishment of these signs is partly due to identifying them too much with the abstract concepts theologians and philosophers have formulated in their regard, uprooting them from the vital substrate in the collective unconscious, which always observes in nature the vast and incomprehensible realm that belongs to reality, a function of which the individual substance expresses. Bread in the hands of Christ is food—the earth become nourishment. The "food" function of the real is expressed in bread that is eaten and achieves its full manifestation in Christ who is food—the bread come down from heaven.

It is necessary, therefore, to make a clear distinction between the vital reality of the substance, with the sacred sign it expresses, and all the theories that can be formulated around the symbol to explain and interpret it. In this way, we will return to experiencing the Christian sacramental signs creatively, poetically. One of the greatest misfortunes in Christianity has been the fall of the lofty liturgy into the hands of little rubricists, mediocre grammarians who have not observed the majestic wave of life that flows through the sacred signs.

By restoring the sacramental symbols to their vital origins and re-examining them in the extensive light of all human religious meaning, perhaps we will recover the lost key to the sacred signs. We will surely have a stronger and more passionate love for the substances of life, which we will find liberated and made holy again by Christ.

This is the work of great poets; in their absence, we must be silent and wait in hope.[7]

Responsory

v. I have a food to eat
   of which you do not know.
r. *I have a food to eat
   of which you do not know.*
v. My food is to do the will of him who sent me.
r. *Food which you do not know.*
v. Glory to the Father, to the Son and to the Holy Spirit.
r. *I have a food to eat
   of which you do not know.*

Intercessions

Let us pray to the Lord Jesus Christ, that he may always send us the Holy Spirit, and let us ask:

Lord, send your Spirit upon us.

Lord Jesus, send your Spirit, the consoler:
—his presence reveals to us the truth of things, fleeting and everlasting, passing and permanent.

Your Spirit shows us the conquests of the mind:
—he introduces us to the life of contemplation, in which our restless hearts find peace.

Your Spirit enlightens our minds:
—he makes us attentive to your Word and docile to your silent presence.

O Lord, we want to understand more and more that the Consoler Spirit is life:
—he frees us from dry doctrines.

His gifts are not words:
—with his power he makes all believers living stones of your house.

May your Spirit sing in us a new song, a song born of pure hearts:
—the song of people who have rediscovered the divine image and likeness.

Prayer

O Lord, you have come:
give us the grace to recognize you.
O Lord, you have spoken:
give us the grace of silence, so we may listen to you.
Come again, O Lord,
we want to welcome you into our home,
we want to open our doors to you,
who live and reign forever and ever. Amen.

(Sing an appropriate closing hymn.)

Prayer to Mary

(optional)

Will the miracle still be possible—
this wonderful exchange of love?
To be the earth that welcomes the Spirit
—to conceive the Word ourselves!

At least you believed, Mary!
We have been wearied by many fables;
troubling idols invade our hearts:
may your faith guide us to the light!

"O children, listen and you will be blessed:
it is the Wisdom of God speaking to you,
a God who watches at the door of your heart
and only waits for each one to open to him.

Blessed are all who follow the way
and are always listening:
those who discover God will have life
and obtain his salvation!"

8

Eucharist: Presence of the Invisible

We have only actions, words and things to make present the reality in which we believe and to which we want to cling with our whole being. Jesus chose bread and wine to indicate in a concrete and viable way his presence in every age, accessible for communion with each person, even beyond rational awareness— to be our new, perceptible essence.

The words he joined to the bread and wine together with the gesture of breaking and distributing the bread—even to the "son of perdition"—do not explain the concealed contents of the signs, nor are they a magic formula that makes strange things happen to the human consciousness and will. Rather, they create the complete human reality, soul-spirit-body, for repeated in the consciousness of the believer, they activate transforming energies.

Gathered in the unity of the one bread and the one wine, people become visible signs, mediations of Christ's unique mediation, of invisible Love, of inexhaustible salvation, a gratuitous gift for a boundless new Life.

Invitation to Prayer

v. Truly you are a hidden God,
r. God of Israel, the savior.
v. God, no one has seen you:
r. The only-begotten Son,
   who is in the bosom of the Father, has revealed you.
v. When he will be manifested
r. We will be like him.

(Sing an appropriate opening hymn.)

Prayer

O God, you remain hidden and mysterious to us,
always beyond the limits of our minds
and the poverty of our feelings;
grant that we may not confuse you
with the image of you that our senses expect.
May we always search for your face
imprinted within the people and things you created.
Through our Lord Jesus Christ, your Son,
who is God and lives and reigns with you
in the unity of the Holy Spirit
forever and ever. Amen.

Reading

If the dispensation of death, carved in letters on stone, came with such splendor that the Israelites could not look at Moses' face because of its brightness, fading as this was, will not the dispensation of the Spirit be attended with greater splendor? For if there was splendor in the dispensation of condemnation, the dispensation of righteousness must far exceed it in splendor. Indeed, in this case, what once had splendor has come to have no splendor at all, because of the splendor that surpasses it. For if what faded away came with splendor, what is permanent must have much more splendor.

Since we have such a hope, we are very bold, not like Moses, who put a veil over his face so that the Israelites might not see the end of the fading splendor. But their minds were hardened; for to this day, when they read the old covenant, that same veil remains unlifted, because only through Christ is it taken away. Yes, to this day whenever Moses is read a veil lies over their minds; but when a man turns to the Lord the veil is removed. Now the Lord is the Spirit, and where the Spirit of the Lord is, there is freedom. And we all, with unveiled face, beholding the glory of the Lord, are being changed into his likeness from one degree of glory to another; for this comes from the Lord who is the Spirit (2 Cor 3:7-18).

Psalm 42

As the deer pants for streams of water,
so my soul pants for you, O God.
My soul thirsts for God, for the living God.
When can I go and meet with God?
My tears have been my food
day and night,
while men say to me all day long,
"Where is your God?"
These things I remember
as I pour out my soul:
how I used to go with the multitude,
leading the procession to the house of God,

with shouts of joy and thanksgiving
among the festive throng.
Why are you downcast, O my soul?
Why so disturbed within me?
Put your hope in God,
for I will yet praise him,
my Savior and my God.
My soul is downcast within me;
therefore I will remember you
from the land of the Jordan,
the heights of Hermon—from Mount Mizar.
Deep calls to deep
in the roar of your waterfalls;
all your waves and breakers
have swept over me.
By day the Lord directs his love,
at night his song is with me—
a prayer to the God of my life.
I say to God, my Rock,
"Why have you forgotten me?
Why must I go about mourning,
oppressed by the enemy?"
My bones suffer mortal agony
as my foes taunt me,
saying to me all day long,
"Where is your God?"
Why are you downcast, O my soul?
Why so disturbed within me?
Put your hope in God,
for I will yet praise him,
my Savior and my God.

With full hearts, O Jesus, we sing to you:
only someone who sees you, already sees the Father;
you said: come and drink,
and living waters will quench your thirst:
you through the Spirit are the truest temple!

Gospel

That very day two of them were going to a village named Emmaus, about seven miles from Jerusalem, and talking with each other about all these things that had happened. While they were talking and discussing together, Jesus himself drew near and went with them. But their eyes were kept from recognizing him. And he said to them, "What is this conversation which you are holding with each other as you walk?" And they stood still, looking sad. Then one of them, named Cleopas, answered him, "Are you the only visitor to Jerusalem who does not know the things that have happened there in these days?" And he said to them, "What things?" And they said to him, "Concerning Jesus of Nazareth, who was a prophet mighty in deed and word before God and all the people, and how our chief priests and rulers delivered him up to be condemned to death, and crucified him. But we have hoped that he was the one to redeem Israel. Yes, and besides all this, it is now the third day since this happened. Moreover, some women of our company amazed us. They were at the tomb early in the morning and did not find his body; and they came back saying that they had even seen a vision of angels, who said that he was alive. Some of those who were with us went to the tomb, and found it just as the women had said; but him they did not see." And he said to them, "O foolish men, and slow of heart to believe all that the prophets have spoken! Was it not necessary that the Christ should suffer these things and enter into his glory?" And beginning with Moses and all the prophets, he interpreted to them in all the scriptures the things concerning himself.

So they drew near to the village to which they were going. He appeared to be going further, but they constrained him, saying, "Stay with us, for it is toward evening and the day is now far spent." So he went in to stay with them. When he was at table with them, he took the bread and blessed, and broke it, and gave it to them. And their eyes were opened and they recognized him; and he vanished out of their sight. They said to each other, "Did not our hearts burn within us while he talked to us on the road, while he opened to us the scriptures?" And they rose that same hour and returned to Jerusalem; and they found the eleven gathered together and those who were with them, who said, "The Lord has risen indeed, and has appeared to Simon!" Then they told what had happened on the road, and how he was known to them in the breaking of the bread (Lk 24:13-35).

Meditation

"Recognition of the Lord Jesus in the sacramental mystery of the shared bread opens another and new phase in the dynamic. Without delay (cf. Lk 24:33), Cleopas and his companion return to Jerusalem, fortified by the energy acquired in eating that bread.

"The gift received in the breaking of the bread inspires the disciples, in their turn, to give what they have experienced. Even more, the strength of the gift impels them in regained confidence to be leaven in the rising dough. They are resurrected, like their Lord. They have passed from sadness to joy (vv. 17, 32), from discouragement to mission (vv. 13, 33), from dispersion to communion (vv. 13, 36).

"The Eucharist urgently calls us to transcend the attitude, 'has been celebrated.' The Eucharist opens itself to all possible times of daily life, where one can and must discover those who consume the bread of sadness or consolation, the bread of pain or peace, or even those whose lives are dramatically deprived of bread.

"'This is my body,' pronounced over the Eucharistic bread, sends the Christian back again to 'this is my body' pronounced over all people—one's brothers and sisters.

"This is the theology that Paul applies in 1 Corinthians 11. One cannot recognize the *Eucharistic body* of Christ without recognizing his *ecclesial body*. One is guilty of 'profaning the body and blood of the Lord,' one 'eats and drinks judgment upon himself,' if one is 'unworthy' of the Eucharistic body of Christ, if he or she is like those Corinthians who 'despise the church of God and humiliate' the members of his body, especially 'those who have nothing.' The guilt lies not in having confused the Eucharistic bread with other food, but with not having appreciated the necessity of receiving the body of Christ in a fitting manner.

"The reference of Eucharistic communion to fraternal communion, therefore, is not only a moral obligation but a theological necessity. One cannot understand the sacramental presence of Christ in the Eucharist without making his *presence in the celebrating assembly* the point of departure. The Church is always the primary reality.

"Thus, Paul emphasizes with a kind of *dogmatic insistence* the truth of what is effected at the Lord's supper: 'The bread which we break, is it not a participation in the body of Christ?' (1 Cor 10:16).

"In the same way, he insists on uniting this declaration with a moral imperative: how can someone participate in the one Eucharistic bread without sharing one's own bread with those who form 'one body' with us? (1 Cor 10:17)."[8]

This guiding rule for the dynamic of this sacrament is weighed down by the entreaties of a universe of unfamiliar and unknown faces: "I was hungry and you gave me food, I was thirsty and you gave me drink, I was a stranger and you welcomed me, I was naked and you clothed me, I was sick and you visited me, I was in prison and you came to me" (Mt 25:35-36). I believe, however, that another aspect must be added to this—an aspect equally fundamental and proper to Christian logic: I must be bread.

Perhaps this is the consequence that is most harmonious with the Eucharist; certainly it is the most difficult. Giving something of ourselves, even sharing faith-experiences, sharing bread, can cost much in terms of overcoming obstacles and difficulties, but it can be done. To love to the end: not to give bread, but to *be myself* bread that nourishes, this is the radical and simple requirement of the mystery of the bread. Not only to have wheat, but to *be* bread that is broken to be eaten—this is the radical consequence of "do this in memory of me."[9]

Responsory

v. The Father who is in me accomplishes his works.
r. *The Father who is in me accomplishes his works.*
v. The Spirit of truth dwells with you and will be in you:
r. *accomplishing his works.*
v. Glory to the Father, to the Son and to the Holy Spirit.
r. *The Father who is in me accomplishes his works.*

Intercessions

To the Lord Jesus Christ, who became a pilgrim on our way so that we might meet him, we lift up our prayer as did the disciples of Emmaus and say:

Stay with us, Lord, because it is almost evening.

Stay with us, Lord, because it is almost evening:
—stay with us and with all your Church.

Stay with us till the end of the day:
—till the end of life, till the end of the world.

Stay with us when the night of doubt approaches:
—the night of fear and of misery and of temptation, the night of bitter death.

Stay among us in your sacrament and in your word:
—with your blessing and your peace.

Stay with us and with all we love:
—in time and in eternity.

Prayer

O supreme Lord, O sole Reality, O true Knowledge,
O enduring Unity,
grant that we may not confine
our faith in you
to the consoling certainty
of having you close bodily,
without seeing anything else
without understanding anything else.
Help us to enlarge our spirits
so that we may recognize you
in every form of life in which you express yourself.
Through Christ our Lord. Amen.

(Sing an appropriate closing hymn.)

Prayer to Mary

(optional)

A girl teaches us how to respond:
how to speak with the hidden God
whom we await and seek forever,
with great anguish of heart, forever!

It was the living and enraptured silence,
the devout silence of all things;
it was prayer that united the centuries,
the most ancient desire of the world.

For you have found grace, O Mary,
as no one else before the eyes of God:
nor were you disturbed by the vision of the angel,
though that greeting vibrates the heavens.

We, so puffed up by our knowledge,
are the angels of only sad announcements,
neither expert in listening as he was,
nor ready to respond as were you!

9

Eucharist: Living in Praise

Bread is the image of gratuitous giving. Its fragrant presence in our homes recalls the desire for unity, the savor of tenderness, the life we would like to experience daily. The breaking of bread reveals the joy of sharing and an inner certitude that impels us to overcome difficult interior and exterior relationships. To be able to break bread every day is to hope to exist not by means of an ephemeral substance, but by means of the true substance that renders our experience of life internally free and externally faithful. To introduce into our life the spirit of the Eucharist that has been celebrated, means to place at the center of our being the mystery the Eucharist contains, as energy generating an authentic response in our way of life. "Eucharist" means "thanksgiving." Our daily pilgrimage assumes, therefore, a continuity of praise, celebrated in everything that we are, make and experience, even in sufferings and contradictions.

Invitation to Prayer

v. Praise overflows from my heart to the Lord:
I want to tell your marvels:
*r. Your glory inspires me to dance
and sing to your name, O Most High.*
v. It is beautiful to praise the Lord:
*r. To announce your love in the morning,
your fidelity in the night.*
v. As long as life lasts, I want to sing
r. Hymns to my God as long as I live.

(Sing an appropriate opening hymn.)

Prayer

O God, who know how to obtain praise
from the mouths of children and infants.
Make our lives simple and humble
and grant that our soul may be only a song of love
to the glory of your name.
Through our Lord Jesus Christ, your Son, who is God
and lives and reigns with you in the unity of the Holy Spirit
forever and ever. Amen.

Reading

Rejoice in the Lord always; again I will say, Rejoice. Let all men know your forbearance. The Lord is at hand. Have no anxiety about anything, but in everything by prayer and supplication with thanksgiving let your requests be made known to God. And the peace of God, which passes all understanding, will keep your hearts and your minds in Christ Jesus.

Finally, brethren, whatever is true, whatever is honorable, whatever is just, whatever is pure, whatever is lovely, whatever is gracious, if there is any excellence, if there is anything worthy of praise, think about these things (Phil 4:4-8).

Psalm 100

Shout for joy to the Lord, all the earth.
Worship the Lord with gladness;
Come before him with joyful songs.
Know that the Lord is God.
It is he who made us, and we are his;
we are his people, the sheep of his pasture.
Enter his gates with thanksgiving
and his courts with praise;
give thanks to him and praise his name.
For the Lord is good and his love endures forever;
his faithfulness continues through all generations.

Chosen race, royal nation,
priests and prophets,
you are the glory of Christ the Lord.

Gospel

He said to his disciples, "Therefore I tell you, do not be anxious about your life, what you shall eat, nor about your body, what you shall put on. For life is more than food, and the body more than clothing. Consider the ravens: they neither sow nor reap, they have neither storehouse nor barn, and yet God feeds them. Of how much more value are you than the birds! And which of you by being anxious can add a cubit to his span of life? If then you are not able to do as small a thing as that, why are you anxious about the rest? Consider the lilies, how they grow; they neither toil nor spin; yet I tell you, even Solomon in all his glory was not arrayed like one of these. But if God so clothes the grass which is alive in the field today and tomorrow is thrown into the oven, how much more will he clothe you, O men of little faith! And do not seek what you are to eat and what you are to drink, nor be of anxious mind. For all the nations of the world seek these things; and your Father knows that you need them. Instead, seek his kingdom, and these things shall be yours as well.

"Fear not, little flock, for it is your Father's good pleasure to give you the kingdom" (Lk 12:22-32).

Meditation

Meditation enables us to discover the face of God, not only in the words of Scripture, but also in the things of the world. The words of Scripture, in fact, do not speak to us of God-in-himself, but of the God who enters into relationship with us through the things of this world and through our neighbor. Thus, the words of Scripture speak to us of the things of the world as God's creatures. The words of Scripture and the things of the world, including our neighbors and ourselves, with all our thoughts and our problems, are indissolubly joined to God. In a certain way, everything speaks to our consciousness. All things are gifts and appeals that God sends us; thus, through the continual changes of history, he invites us to manifest a life conformed to his will. So, we are called to a continuous maturation and a spiritual growth toward an ever greater understanding of the wealth of God's thoughts and the depth of his love for us. We are called to love him more and to unite ourselves more intimately with him.

Eucharist: Living in Praise

The complexity of different situations and problems emphasizes the inexhaustible and infinite meaning of things and persons thrusting their roots into the infinity of God himself. The more we fathom the meaning of things and persons, the more we can discover an ever deeper meaning in Scripture and vice versa. In the continually deeper search into these two kinds of revelation, we advance in the perception of the infinite love of God that touches our hearts to the point of tears. Without a doubt, we can see things and persons in a superficial way. We do this when we look at them only to possess or enjoy them; when the desire to dominate them becomes the source of infinite preoccupations. This was why the fathers spoke of the necessity of freeing ourselves from preoccupations and anxieties about obtaining things or meeting persons. But they certainly did not intend to manifest contempt for the creatures of God; rather, they wanted to show the necessity of learning how to look at all the creatures of God with pure eyes, considering them as divine words in the very heart of things, as ways by which God wants us to rise up to him.

We are asked, then, not to abstain from things in themselves, but to truly love things and persons, to be able to see them in their meaning and ontological reality, which is rooted in the thought and creative action of God himself. Then our gaze, thus purified, will no longer stop at the things and persons, but will reach beyond to God, who reveals himself through them, and we will discover that God has given them to us in his love for us so that we too may grow in love.

The love of God within us acquires a purifying energy in regard to our relationships with things and with other persons. God cannot be enclosed in only one person; he cannot be confined by anything or anyone. He gives himself only in the measure in which each one welcomes him in communion with all other beings. So, approaching God and opening ourselves to his presence means purifying ourselves, so that in God we may see things and persons beyond their limits and be in communion with them.

As a means for seeing things with pure eyes, the ascetic St. Mark recommends immediately offering to Christ as a sacrifice any image that enters our minds. To make such an offering means to enter into the most intimate and profound part of our being. It is here, after Baptism, that Christ lives.

Our journey, then, consists of three phases: to think of everything "according to truth," that is, in a disinterested way; to offer it all to Christ and, through him, to everyone he loves; to seek the deep center of our being and allow it to emerge in all our thoughts—in short, to make it always present.

To offer God the image of everything or of everyone we think of, is to thank God for this thing or person, either to glorify him or to ask his help in performing the service requested or required of us.[10]

Responsory

v. I have glorified you by accomplishing the work
that you gave me to do.
r. I have glorified you by accomplishing the work
that you gave me to do.
v. I have made your name known to them.
r. Accomplishing the work
that you gave me to do.
v. Glory to the Father, to the Son and to the Holy Spirit.
r. I have glorified you by accomplishing the work
that you gave me to do.

Eucharist: Living in Praise

Intercessions

We direct our prayer in the Spirit to the Father of all mercy, who listens with goodness to the requests of his children, and we exclaim:

You, O Lord, are our life and salvation!

The praise of your entire Church rises up to you, O Father:
—purify our lips, so that our song may be pleasing to you and unite itself to the harmony of all your creation.

In you, O Father, we have placed our hope, because only in you can our searching hearts find peace:
—calm the yearning for the infinite which continually spurs us onward.

Without your help, O Father, the works of our hands are not life-giving, nor are we able to offer a ray of hope:
—help us in our insufficiency and expand the narrowness within us toward the infinite spaces to which your love calls us.

Remember, O Father, those who are oppressed by others, those whom our selfishness continues to exclude, those whom our little faith alienates from the joy of believing:
—reveal yourself to everyone as a loving Father and enlighten our eyes, so that we may see your living presence in all people.

Prayer

O Father, you wanted
to dwell within us by your Holy Spirit.
Grant that our entire life
may be a song of praise to your love.
Keep far away the snares of the ancient enemy,

so that all our thoughts and actions
may be conformed to your will,
which you revealed in Jesus Christ, who is God
and lives and reigns forever and ever. Amen.

(Sing an appropriate closing hymn.)

Prayer to Mary

(optional)

Already then a mother—
bearing the seed within her womb,
bringing spring to the hills of Judea,
the new time awaited by the world—

Mary said: "My soul glorifies the Lord,
my spirit exults with joy."
This is life, nothing else, O Mother.
Open our hearts to your secret.

As dialogue with heaven inebriates us
and grace revives us,
so the most humble can sing
and fill their solitude!

Glory to the Father, to the Son and to the Holy Spirit,
source of joy for the life of the heart—
the life that floods the Virgin Mother—
glory to her, for she prays and sings.

10

Eucharist: Living in Peace

"*Lamb of God, you take away the sins of the world: grant us peace.*"

We pray this before the breaking of the bread—but not to create a sentiment that momentarily harmonizes with the peaceful presence of the bread we eat. Rather, we pray to profess a state brought about in each and in all by the unique sacrifice that, in its total and inexplicable violence has set limits to every division and desire to condemn.

If you believe that the "lamb," meek and humble of heart, has truly made the "ultimate enemy" powerless and has driven him off, how can you dare to define anyone as an "enemy"?

Even more, if you do not wish to be a pagan, a senseless disciple of empty idols, you must pray for those who in some way your weakness still defines as "enemy." You can do so only if you can experience the enchanting desire in peace—that is, with a total calming of your energies, reconciled and made fruitful by the divine dream that integrates all means of violence through a strenuous and attentive commitment to accepting others generously.

Invitation to Prayer

v. O God, you assure peace to the people.
r. *Peace because they hope and trust in you.*
v. Have the same feelings as one another; live in peace.
r. *And the God of love and peace will be with you.*
v. Render to no one evil for evil.
r. *Live in peace with everyone.*

(Sing an appropriate opening hymn.)

Prayer

Father,
send your gift of peace into our hearts.
You know our efforts to follow
the trail that Jesus has blazed before us.
Forgive our weakness and infidelity,
so that, reinvigorated by your Spirit of peace,
we may resume our journey with greater courage,
until we reach the home where you await us.
Through our Lord Jesus Christ,
your Son, who is God,
and lives and reigns with you
in the unity of the Holy Spirit
forever and ever. Amen.

Reading

I...a prisoner for the Lord, beg you to lead a life worthy of the calling to which you have been called, with all lowliness and meekness, with patience, forbearing one another in love, eager to maintain the unity of the Spirit in the bond of peace. There is one body and one Spirit, just as you were called to the one hope that belongs to your call, one Lord, one faith, one baptism, one God and Father of us all, who is above all and through all and in all (Eph 4:1-6).

Psalm 122

I rejoiced with those who said to me,
"Let us go to the house of the Lord."
Our feet are standing
within your gates, O Jerusalem.
Jerusalem is built like a city
that is closely compacted together.
That is where the tribes go up,
the tribes of the Lord,
to praise the name of the Lord
according to the statute given to Israel.
There the thrones for judgment stand,
the thrones of the house of David.
Pray for the peace of Jerusalem:
"May those who love you be secure.
May there be peace within your walls
and security within your citadels."
For the sake of my brothers and friends,
I will say, "Peace be within you."
For the sake of the house of the Lord our God,
I will seek your prosperity.

Fellow citizens of the saints, brothers and sisters,
O family of God, sing to the city
that comes down from heaven
as a bride prepared for the wedding!

Gospel

"You have heard that it was said, 'An eye for an eye and a tooth for a tooth.' But I say to you, Do not resist one who is evil. But if anyone strikes you on the right cheek, turn to him the other also; and if anyone would sue you and take your coat, let him have your cloak as well; and if anyone forces you to go one mile, go with him two miles. Give to him who begs from you, and do not refuse him who would borrow from you.

"You have heard that it was said, 'You shall love your neighbor and hate your enemy.' But I say to you, Love your enemies and pray for those who persecute you, so that you may be sons of your Father who is in heaven; for he makes his sun rise on the evil and on the good, and sends rain on the just and on the unjust. For if you love those who love you, what reward have you? Do not even the tax collectors do the same? And if you salute only your brethren, what more are you doing than others? Do not even the Gentiles do the same? You, therefore, must be perfect, as your heavenly Father is perfect" (Mt 5:38-48).

Meditation

To say "Eucharist" is to say: "the sacrament of unity and peace for the entire universe." In this sacrament anxiety about created things is calmed. All the expectations of the spirit are met. It is like the restlessness of the poet who finds peace by losing himself in the infinite:

> "and so amidst this immensity
> I drown my thought
> and shipwreck is sweet to me in this sea."

To say "peace" is the same as saying: "the tranquillity of order"—order in the greatest and broadest meaning—in the sense of harmony, and therefore, of truth and beauty together; in the sense of the fulfillment of every desire, of the perfection of humanity. It is self-realization according to the divine ideal, the most universal and demanding ideal—an ideal that always transcends us, by which peace is always a utopia, the ultimate value of the world, as is the Eucharist itself.

Peace is certainly better that a cease-fire, and it is more than not killing or destroying. It is reaching out and grasping the hand of a friend and brother or sister, showing not only that the hand is disarmed, but the heart as well. It is the squeezing of the hand to express affection, the sharing of pain and joy, the intertwining of lives. Peace means having a heart as large as the world, a heart in which no one ever feels marginalized or even less, excluded. According to such a heart, all people have equal rights and equal responsibilities and every person is sacred. The salvation of each one is a guarantee of the salvation of all. Peace means that we do not need to be rich or poor, slave or free, man or woman. This is even more true for Christians, because we become one reality in the Lord. We are in Christ to speak to the universe about values that are recognized by all according to human nature, according to the utopia that the world dreams will come about. But that utopia expects each one of us to bring it about, for everything depends on us![11]

Responsory

v. I leave you peace, I give you my peace.
r. I leave you peace, I give you my peace.
v. Not as the world gives
r. I give you my peace.
v. Glory to the Father, to the Son and to the Holy Spirit.
r. I leave you peace, I give you my peace.

Intercessions

We turn our prayer in the Spirit to the Father of all mercy, who graciously listens to the pleas of his children, and we ask:

Send us your light and your peace.

O Lord, help us to be people of peace
—if there is no peace in us, we will not give peace; if there is no order in us, we will not create order.

O Lord, revive our efforts
—to meet you in everyone who will fill our day.

Help us to discover the field you have entrusted to our labor:
—help us to love it and bring order to it.

May our journey be a sign of life and beauty:
—like the flight of doves traversing the sky.

Teach us that we belong to others:
—so that the happiness of others may be our only thought.

May our lips sing the new song
—of a heart freed by you, O Lord.

Prayer

Father,
give us perfect, disinterested peace—
peace that makes your presence
and your intervention effective—
peace that conquers all bad will,
all darkness.
Through Christ our Lord. Amen.

(Sing an appropriate closing hymn.)

Prayer to Mary

(optional)

Blessing to you, daughter of Zion,
highly favored by our God:
you are ever cared for by the Lord,
O creation full of grace.

His holy face shines upon you;
the Lord has always turned toward you
his favorable and peaceful gaze;
peace has chosen you for its dwelling.

Blessing to you from Israel
who bears its new name, Mary.
Jerusalem was just an image
of which you were the splendid dawn.

11

Eucharist: Living in Expectation

To celebrate the Eucharist is not only to remember what the Lord Jesus has done for our salvation. It is also "to remember" the future—the full and perfect enjoyment of the realities celebrated and of what we will ultimately be. Although the future is the object of the profession of faith, it must necessarily become "martyrdom"—witness in concrete existence of the truths that are known. Thus, the future is not distant in time, but the truest form of the present. In it we experience the creative fascination of the Word proclaimed to the mind and penetrating the waiting heart. We experience the patient fulfillment of the promises, the presence stronger than any other sensible presence, of which it is the unforeseen and astounding foundation—the presence of him who is always "coming" and therefore "with us until the end of the world."

To live in expectation, then, is the first consequence, or rather the continuation in life, of the Eucharistic encounter. It is almost an "unveiling" of the reality that is "veiled" in the celebration.

Invitation to Prayer

v. Only in God is my soul at rest,
r. From him comes my hope.
v. I am consumed in the expectation of salvation.
r. I hope in your word.
v. We await new heavens and a new earth.
r. In which justice will have a secure dwelling.

(Sing an appropriate opening hymn.)

Prayer

O Lord, grant us the strength,
the patience, the necessary purity
to await your continuous coming,
to be amazed by your inconceivable revelation,
to contemplate you constantly
and belong to you without shadows or limits.
Through our Lord Jesus Christ, your Son, who is God
and lives and reigns with you in the unity of the Holy Spirit
forever and ever. Amen.

Reading

Rejoice always, pray constantly, give thanks in all circumstances; for this is the will of God in Christ Jesus for you. Do not quench the Spirit, do not despise prophesying, but test everything; hold fast what is good, abstain from every form of evil.

May the God of peace himself sanctify you wholly; and may your spirit and soul and body be kept sound and blameless at the coming of our Lord Jesus Christ. He who calls you is faithful, and he will do it (1 Thess 5:16-24).

Psalm 130

Out of the depths I cry to you, O Lord;
O Lord, hear my voice.
Let your ears be attentive
to my cry for mercy.
If you, O Lord, kept a record of sins,
O Lord, who could stand?
But with you there is forgiveness;
therefore you are feared.
I wait for the Lord, my soul waits,
and in his word I put my hope.
My soul waits for the Lord
more than watchmen wait for the morning,
more than watchmen wait for the morning.
O Israel, put your hope in the Lord,
for with the Lord is unfailing love
and with him is full redemption.
He himself will redeem Israel
from all their sins.

To his throne of grace and love
he has opened the way for everyone:
Let us go to the Father with confidence,
And may the Spirit sing through us.

Gospel

"The kingdom of heaven shall be compared to ten maidens who took their lamps and went to meet the bridegroom. Five of them were foolish, and five were wise. For when the foolish took their lamps, they took no oil with them; but the wise took flasks of oil with their lamps. As the bridegroom was delayed, they all slumbered and slept. But at midnight there was a cry, 'Behold, the bridegroom! Come out to meet him.' Then all those maidens rose and trimmed their lamps. And the foolish said to the wise, 'Give us some of your oil, for our lamps are going out.' But the wise replied, 'Perhaps there will not be enough for us and for you; go rather to the dealers and buy for yourselves.' And while they went to buy, the bridegroom came, and those who were ready went in with him to the marriage feast; and the door was shut. Afterward the other maidens came also, saying, 'Lord, lord, open to us.' But he replied, 'Truly, I say to you, I do not know you.' Watch, therefore, for you know neither the day nor the hour" (Mt 25:1-12).

Meditation

It is not easy for experts to explain how life begins, but even the non-expert can say that it begins as sleep begins—in continuity with, but also different from, all the preparations and attempts that precede it. Sleep gives meaning to all those preparations and attempts. If sleep does not come, everything is reduced to the absurd nocturnal liturgy of the insomniac. Sleep, then, contrary to appearances and even to a certain mentality found in the Bible, is a way of manifesting life, not a sign or anticipation of death. So true is this that the most intense and profound way a man and woman can be together is called "sleeping together." This is not only a euphemism.

Sleeping together, it is completely natural for a man and a woman who love one another to create a new life. This is something totally different from the simple will to bring a child into being.

Thus does the kingdom of God come into being—through a certain initial state of sleep and beatitude, which is not a preface to death, but a beginning of life.

In this way, we approach the meaning of "seek *first* the kingdom of God." We are not to worry about preparations for sleep, nor to be concerned with various efforts; we are to seek the sleep itself, waiting for it patiently. It is near.

The kingdom of God does not come by an act of the will, but in the sleep that is always blessed by love.

Like the maternal womb, so the bread of heaven is not so much a conscious memory as an acquired tranquillity, a received peace, security, a grace from which life draws both earnestness and endless blessing. How useless to squeeze fervor into Eucharistic fervorinos!

What havoc one makes of the beatitudes when they are separated from that ambient of happiness and grace which were the lips of Jesus when he pronounced them! Even the Gospel clearly says that people remained spellbound because of the words of grace that issued from his mouth. Here we could apply in all its realism that thesis of dogmatic theology according to which Jesus enjoyed the "beatific vision" during his entire lifetime, not excluding the passion.

The beatitudes are such, therefore, because Jesus was blessed from his mother's breast to his Father's breast. He could not fail to translate into his life and words this great tranquillity, security, balance and joy.

Gathered together, pronounced by persons who have a totally different past, the beatitudes become like flowers plucked from the earth and placed in a vase. Before, they were incomparable; now, they have become at best a series of good paradoxes used as an opiate of the people.

We can no longer play like children with the words of the Gospel. Either we share with Jesus the blessedness of children of the Father, or all our efforts to project blessedness into the future will undoubtedly be compensatory, uneasy and anxious. These characteristics will strike our audience prior to and more strongly than our profession of faith in heaven. How sad it is when preaching about heaven is not based on a happy past. On the other hand, if one's past was happy, there is little need to say much about future happiness, because one possesses a pledge, first-fruits, a down-payment.[12]

Responsory

v. Keep watch and pray so as not to enter into temptation.
r. Keep watch and pray so as not to enter into temptation.
v. Be ready, with your belt around your waist
and your lantern lighted
r. So as not to enter into temptation.
v. Glory to the Father, to the Son and to the Holy Spirit.
r. Keep watch and pray so as not to enter into temptation.

Intercessions

Let us direct our petitions to the Lord Jesus Christ. He is our mediator with the Father, so we say:

Lord, we pray to you.

O Christ, you are the sign for us that human history has a future, and that we are not alone in time:
—be our guide this day which your love has given us.

We want to walk with you, Lord:
—help us to understand that the cross was not given us to look at, but to carry behind you.

Eucharist: Living in Expectation 131

Always give us more faith and more joy:
—give us courage; help us understand that faith is dead without the courage of deeds.

Grant that our hands may respect all creatures:
—may our ears be attentive to hear your voice.

Grant that we may always be ready to meet you with clean hands and pure eyes:
—when the light fades at sunset, may we come to you without shame.

Prayer

O Father, may neither earthly goods
nor easy successes seduce us,
nor death frighten us;
but may your Spirit enlighten our eyes
to distinguish the ephemeral from the eternal,
the passing from the permanent,
so that we may share
the banquet of endless life with you,
who are the origin of all things.
Through Christ our Lord. Amen.

(Sing an appropriate closing hymn.)

Prayer to Mary

(optional)

The root is still ready to flower:
Mary, you are the image of the Church.
Humanity always generates him;
the shoot of Jesse is ready to bud forth:

"He who always blooms in the sun"—
this is his name sung in the psalm.
We announce this to all the earth
so that all may take hope again.

Christ, we are always waiting for you,
like the earth and the things that you make new
so too, you renew us every day:
may all see your salvation.

12

Eucharist: Essence of Creation

*I*n *his self-giving, the Lord Jesus consumed the form of his historical and earthly presence. Then he placed himself under the form of bread and wine, so that everyone might eat and drink of him and live.*

Having drawn all things to himself in his experience of death, he has become the source of a creation whose goodness and beauty are based on a harmonious balance stemming from the reconciliation achieved by him and accomplished in him.

The person who nourishes himself on the life-giving and substantial food that is the body and blood of Christ, acquires a consciousness of being rooted in Christ Jesus. This consciousness becomes the life-giving center of all ones human resources— which, clothed with new light, constitute the identity of the person "conformed to the image of the Son."

The person becomes a radiant power in the cosmos of that life-giving substance progressively taking up its dwelling in him.

Humbly giving his energies to this Eucharistic presence, he collaborates with God's great and marvelous work for the unity of all.

Invitation to Prayer

v. You are the true source of life,
r. In your light we see light.
v. You form the world.
r. And everything the world contains.
v. You are the designer of all salvation,
r. Forged in the heart of the earth.
(Sing an appropriate opening hymn.)

Prayer

Lord of all that is,
you are the unity of everything,
the essential origin of every living thing.
Let our most ardent desire
be to nourish ourselves with your very life
until we reach perfect union with you.
Through our Lord Jesus Christ,
your Son who is God,
and lives and reigns with you
in the unity of the Holy Spirit
forever and ever. Amen.

Reading

[Christ] is the image of the invisible God, the first-born of all creation; for in him all things were created, in heaven and on earth, visible and invisible, whether thrones or dominions or principalities or authorities—all things were created through him and for him. He is before all things, and in him all things hold together. He is the head of the body, the church; he is the beginning, the first-born from the dead, that in everything he might be pre-eminent. For in him all the fullness of God was pleased to dwell, and through him to reconcile to himself all things, whether on earth or in heaven, making peace by the blood of his cross (Col 1:15-20).

Psalm 87

He has set his foundation on the holy mountain;
the Lord loves the gates of Zion
more than all the dwellings of Jacob.
Glorious things are said of you,
O city of God:
"I will record Rahab and Babylon
among those who acknowledge me—
Philistia too, and Tyre, along with Cush—
and will say, 'This one was born in Zion.'"
Indeed, of Zion it will be said,
"This one and that one were born in her,
and the Most High himself will establish her."
The Lord will write in the register of the peoples:
"This one was born in Zion."
As they make music they will sing,
"All my fountains are in you."

And Parthians and Medes and Elamites, O Lord,
sing to you in their own languages—
O living Pentecost, your Church!

Gospel

Jesus answered them, "The hour has come for the Son of man to be glorified. Truly, truly, I say to you, unless a grain of wheat falls into the earth and dies, it remains alone; but if it dies, it bears much fruit. He who loves his life loses it, and he who hates his life in this world will keep it for eternal life. If any one serves me, he must follow me; and where I am, there shall my servant be also; if anyone serves me, the Father will honor him.

"Now is my soul troubled. And what shall I say? 'Father, save me from this hour'? No, for this purpose I have come to this hour. Father glorify your name." Then a voice came from heaven, "I have glorified it, and I will glorify it again." The crowd standing by heard it and said that it had thundered. Others said, "An angel has spoken to him." Jesus answered, "This voice has come for your sake, not for mine. Now is the judgment of this world, now shall the ruler of this world be cast out; and I, when I am lifted up from the earth, will draw all men to myself" (Jn 12:23-32).

Meditation

The rethinking of creation in the New Testament and afterwards has moved between the boundaries of the already and the not yet; of the hidden and the manifest; of the seed and its maturation; of human responsibility in hastening or delaying the appearance of a shadowless new world. Everything begins from an irreplaceable presupposition: Jesus is the Lord of cosmic-human creation. This faith is confirmed despite the lack of support of visible things, of verifiable evidence. The testimony of the author of the Letter to the Hebrews is explicit in this regard: "Now in putting everything in subjection to him, he left nothing outside his control. As it is, we do not see everything in subjection to him. But we see Jesus...crowned with glory and honor..." (Heb 2:8-9).

The "seeing" of which the text speaks is the clarity of naked faith, rendered incapable of displaying concrete proofs, for at present these do not exist. Within a culture that continues to make plans as if God and his inheritance did not exist, forgetful or weary of his unimaginable return, there are some who, persuaded by the Spirit (1 Cor 3:2), persist in keeping alive the memory of a singular event placed by God as an eschatological icon of creation and as a spring from which gushes the water of a Spirit who initiates the one who possesses him into the art of dwelling in this creation.

To confess the lordship of Jesus is not to diminish human lordship. It is simply to recognize that there are human beings who say they have already received from him the gift of the new world and have learned from him what creation really needs. It needs a different relationship with God, with self, with others, with things, with suffering and with death. Where this difference begins to appear, the old creation begins to change into the new, in expectation of the final fulfillment. This is to realize the new mandate of stewardship. In regard to God, this newness consists in leaving behind the fear that was typical of the first human beings (Gen 3:10), and living in the divine presence with total trust (Eph 3:12).

The conscience is reawakened to the amazing awareness that one is a dwelling of Light, in which this experience of the absolutely gratuitous becomes a courageous narrative of "gentleness and reverence" (1 Pt 3:15), of absolute non-violence and docility: "We will hear you again about this" (Acts 17:32b). The heavenly Jerusalem is the dwelling of God with humanity and of humanity with God. The things of the past—the fear of God, fear of denying him and fear of forgetting him—are gone. Something new is born: God accompanies humanity (Gen 3:10), walks at our side (Mi 6:8), makes his home in us (Jn 14:23).

Wherever they are found, the friends of God are the real sign of his nearness, the proof that it is possible to recount the event of the God-human relationship in a different way—to begin from the here and now, sustained by a humble opinion of self—for everything is a grace—and by a vivid awareness that everything is hidden: "Your life is hid with Christ in God" (Col 3:3).[13]

Responsory

v. There is only one Lord, Jesus Christ.
   All things exist through him.
r. There is only one Lord, Jesus Christ.
   All things exist through him.
v. He is the eternal source.
r. All things exist through him.
v. Glory to the Father, to the Son and to the Holy Spirit.
r. There is only one Lord, Jesus Christ.
   All things exist through him.

Intercessions

To the Lord Jesus Christ, light of the world, we lift up our prayer and song of praise, for he alone is the source of our life of grace:

To you, Christ, praise and love.

We raise the hymn of our gratitude to the true light, the eternal light, the source of all things:
—may he enlighten us, that our life may be light and joy.

You are pure light:
—uncreated light that gives origin to the universe.

You are the light of every being that comes into existence:
—you are the inner light of each of us.

You are the only one, the first and the last, who opens and closes the doors of life:

Eucharist: Essence of Creation

—the one who commands death, who floods the ways of death with life.

You are the life that frees us from the evil within us human beings:
—to you be our love and the total offering of our being.

You are the glory of creation at the dawn of time:
—may your day shine resplendently in every living thing and proclaim that you are coming soon.

Prayer

Father in heaven,
earth is also a heaven,
and so you are on earth.
You are in each of us, and each of us is in you
in a divine ecstasy, in grace, in support.
Reawaken us, O renewer of consciences,
inflame us with your fire.
Consume us with your heavenly fire.
May we do your will,
may we perfectly and lovingly
do your will.
Through Christ our Lord. Amen.

(Sing an appropriate closing hymn.)

Prayer to Mary

(optional)

Mother, reveal the great source to us,
since you were already in God's plan
when he created things in the Word.

Mother, help us to welcome him,
to clothe him in our flesh,
made fruitful with you by the Spirit.

O Mother, grant that the Church may continue
its prayer of one heart and one soul,
so that the Spirit may continue to descend.

Mother, assist us in the new beginning;
may the whole world understand your words,
and joy return to fill the earth.

O Mother, may there be a perennial Pentecost,
may holy fire devour all evil,
may the Church be as free as the wind.

You are the holy beauty of creation,
the image of the end of time,
the living ark of the One Man.

13

Eucharist: Sacrifice for Life

The Eucharist embodies the most profound and complete meaning of a life offered in sacrifice—that of the Son of God made man, and also that of those who share in the sacred mystery of Christ's body and blood and become an enduring sacrifice, pleasing to God.

This does not involve more bloodshed, nor the martyrdom of oneself or another, but endeavoring with all one's strength to make one's life a "eucharist"—a free remembrance of what has been given to us—which should truly shine in our words and actions, accomplished with a generous will and in a spirit of authentic service. It involves offering life, not death, in praise of the glory of the sole Lord of life.

Invitation to Prayer

v. The Lord is my portion,
r. My cup, my destiny.
v. Only one thing I ask:
r. To dwell in the house of God all the days of my life.
v. You show me the path to walk,
r. So that you may bring me to you.

(Sing an appropriate opening hymn.)

Prayer

O Lord Jesus, free us from being selfishly closed up,
from following passing interests that render our actions fruitless.
Enable us to become living bread like you—
to give ourselves to you
in a joyous consecration of our entire being.
You are God and live and reign with the Father
in the unity of the Holy Spirit
forever and ever. Amen.

Reading

Since the law was but a shadow of the good things to come instead of the true form of these realities, it can never, by the same sacrifices which are continually offered year after year, make perfect those who draw near. Otherwise, would they not have ceased to be offered? If the worshipers had once been cleansed, they would no longer have any consciousness of sin. But in these sacrifices there is a reminder of sin year after year. For it is impossible that the blood of bulls and goats should take away sins.

Consequently, when Christ came into the world, he said,
"Sacrifices and offerings you have not desired,
but a body you have prepared for me;
in burnt offerings and sin offerings
you have taken no pleasure.
Then I said, 'Lo, I have come to do your will, O God,'
as it is written of me in the roll of the book."

When he said above, "You have neither desired nor taken pleasure in sacrifices and offerings and burnt offerings and sin offerings" (these are offered according to the law), then he added, "Lo, I have come to do your will." He abolishes the first in order to establish the second. And by that will we have been sanctified through the offering of the body of Jesus Christ once for all (Heb 10:1-10).

Psalm 40:1-10

I waited patiently for the Lord;
he turned to me and heard my cry.
He lifted me out of the pit,
out of the slimy mud and mire;
he set my feet on a rock
and gave me a firm place to stand.
He put a new song in my mouth,
a hymn of praise to our God.
Many will see and fear
and put their trust in the Lord.
Blessed is the man
who makes the Lord his trust,
who does not look to the proud,
to those who turn aside to false gods.

Many, O Lord my God,
are the wonders you have done.
The things you planned for us
no one can recount to you;
were I to speak and tell of them,
they would be too many to declare.
Sacrifice and offering you did not desire,
but my ears you have pierced;
burnt offerings and sin offerings
you did not require.
Then I said, "Here I am, I have come—
it is written about me in the scroll.
I desire to do your will, O my God;
your law is within my heart."
I proclaim righteousness in the great assembly;
I do not seal my lips, as you know, O Lord.
I do not hide your righteousness in my heart;
I speak of your faithfulness and salvation.
I do not conceal your love and your truth
from the great assembly.

To you, Christ, sent by God
to redeem all creation,
to you, the altar and victim of justice,
we lift our hymn of gratitude and praise.

Gospel

"Truly, truly I say to you, I am the door of the sheep. All who came before me are thieves and robbers; but the sheep did not heed them. I am the door; if any one enters by me, he will be saved, and will go in and out and find pasture. The thief comes only to steal and kill and destroy; I came that they may have life, and have it abundantly. I am the good shepherd. The good shepherd lays down his life for the sheep. He who is a hireling and not a shepherd, whose own the sheep are not, sees the wolf coming and leaves the sheep and flees; and the wolf snatches them and scatters them. He flees because he is a hireling and cares nothing for the sheep. I am the good shepherd; I know my own and my own know me, as the Father knows me and I know the Father; and I lay down my life for the sheep" (Jn 10:7-15).

Meditation

"This is my body, which is given for you"—"This is the new covenant in my blood"—"Do this in remembrance of me"—"Take; eat." At the heart of the great Eucharistic Prayer, through the Spirit, the Father fulfills and actualizes the word of Jesus. The bread and wine are really and truly changed, becoming the presence of the Risen Lord, the Living One. The Lord is present to his own as a word that recalls and as food that communicates itself.

On Sunday, therefore, we remember the Risen One and insist that his memory be kept. We proclaim his death as the interpretation and culmination of his life, his resurrection, his ascension to the right hand of the Father, Pentecost, our expectation of his return. This is both a cultural and an existential remembering, because what is celebrated in the liturgy needs to be lived in history. Become love to the point of giving your life, as a reflection of the Son, who is the image of the Father—and the Father is love. How is it possible to become a presence that forgives, that speaks and lives wisely, that intercedes, that loves to the point of dying to the instinct for self-preservation? How is it possible to think and act like God in Jesus? The answer is to be found in

Communion. Jesus communicates himself, and being "in" him, as the branch is attached to the vine, is the basis of being "like" him. The Risen One gives himself as food to his own and with himself, the Spirit and the Father. The Spirit of love makes the believer and believing community overflow with a life of forgiveness, wisdom, intercession and openness to future dreams, hopes and prayers—a future of joy, light and beauty.

Consequently, the remembrance of God as *agape*, manifested in Jesus and the Spirit of love, communicated by the awaited Living One, orientates the lives of the disciples toward a love that finds its most beautiful and complete gesture in death, as an event of love and as the gateway to the presence of the One who breaks and shatters the last great instinct for self-preservation, making us new creatures like the Risen Son, pure gifts at last, given by the Spirit according to his own measure. Not only has death entered the ambient of immortality; it is the complete destruction of the old person and rebirth of the new person—one who is totally open, bread for the life of humanity. This is the secret that is revealed to us each Sunday by the one who no longer calls us servants but friends, "for all that I have heard from my Father I have made known to you" (Jn 15:15).[14]

Responsory

v. No one has greater love than this:
   to give one's life for one's friends.
r. *No one has greater love than this:*
   to give one's life for one's friends.
v. I have given you an example,
   so that as I have done you also may do:
r. *Give one's life for one's friends.*

v. Glory to the Father, to the Son and to the Holy Spirit.
r. *No one has greater love than this:*
to give one's life for one's friends.

Intercessions

We pray to the Lord Jesus Christ, who loved us to the point of giving his life so that we might become children of his heavenly Father, and we ask:

Lord Jesus, teach us to live united in your name.

We are confused like those who do not know you, like those who find no meaning in life:
—give self-denial and strength to our day.

Help us to live your love, to accomplish your will in the gift of our lives:
—and, through our little gift, we ask you to awaken the dead to the life of the Spirit.

Grant that we may profoundly experience the world's pain:
—may it give us the strength to serve others with ever greater love.

Lord Jesus, reveal yourself and live in us:
—work through us, so that others may know you and live of your life.

Prayer

May our bodies be your instruments;
our wills your handmaids;
our intellects your servants;
and our entire selves be yours!
O God, who lives and reigns forever and ever. Amen.
(Sing an appropriate closing hymn.)

Prayer to Mary

(optional)

They were rare and humble,
the words and voiceless sighs
of him, the living speech of the Father,
the Word who created the worlds.

But in her they had a sad echo,
like the fall of stones upon a tomb,
while she saw the pool of blood
that formed at the foot of the tree.

Surely you thought of the moment
when everything would be fulfilled:
You placed him once again in your womb
to give birth to him anew, O Mary.

Who knows the times, O women,
that you alone gave life to your children,
as if you were the virgin-mother.
In this way the human race continues.

Thus you will be the true image
of this Church forever called
the perennial, life-giving mother,
whose compassion comforts the earth.

14

Eucharist: Calming of Every Desire

"I have earnestly desired to eat this passover with you" (Lk 22:15). According to the evangelist, Jesus said these words before the distribution of the bread and wine at the passover supper that preceded his passion. His ardent desire was consummated with the gesture that prefigured the total gift of himself in obedience to the Father's will.

In the face of such an example, every human desire should decisively direct itself toward freedom and fulfillment in the Father's will. Only this attitude can transform celebration into a sensible life-project. It will lead not to a useless and misdirected battle against the world, the body and other material things, but to a wise activation in concrete experience of desire for the image of God in the human person. Every desire, thus directed and lived through faith in the infinite love of God, results in interior peace that makes the heart an altar for a universal sacrifice of communion and gift.

Invitation to Prayer

v. As a deer longs for running streams,
r. My soul yearns for you, O God.
v. Allow your life to flow into God,
r. Trust in him and he will act.
v. The Lord fills you with grace and sweetness,
r. He satisfies you for many years.

(Sing an appropriate opening hymn.)

Prayer

In you, O Father, fullness of every good,
all our desires and every anxious aspiration find rest.
In the humble form of the bread that you give us
and in the cup of intoxicating wine,
grant that we experience the ecstasy
of your peacemaking presence.
Through our Lord Jesus Christ, your Son, who is God
and lives and reigns with you in the unity of the Holy Spirit
forever and ever. Amen.

Reading

There is therefore now no condemnation for those who are in Christ Jesus. For the law of the Spirit of life in Christ Jesus has set me free from the law of sin and death. For God has done what the law, weakened by the flesh, could not do: sending his own Son in the likeness of sinful flesh and for sin, he condemned sin in the flesh, in order that the just requirement of the law might be fulfilled in us, who walk not according to the flesh but according to the Spirit. For those who live according to the flesh set their minds on the things of the flesh, but those who live according to the Spirit set their minds on the things of the Spirit. To set the mind on the flesh is death, but to set the mind on the Spirit is life and peace. For the mind that is set on the flesh is hostile to God; it does not submit to God's law, indeed it cannot; and those who are in the flesh cannot please God.

But you are not in the flesh, you are in the Spirit, if the Spirit of God really dwells in you. Any one who does not have the Spirit of Christ does not belong to him (Rom 8:1-9).

Psalm 23

The Lord is my shepherd, I shall not be in want.
He makes me lie down in green pastures,
he leads me beside quiet waters, he restores my soul.
He leads me in paths of righteousness
for his name's sake.
Even though I walk
through the valley of the shadow of death,
I will fear no evil;
for you are with me;
your rod and your staff, they comfort me.
You prepare a table before me
in the presence of my enemies.
You anoint my head with oil;
my cup overflows.
Surely goodness and love will follow me
all the days of my life,
and I will dwell in the house of the Lord forever

Thanks be to the Father who has blessed us
in Christ from the dawning of the world:
the one shepherd in the Spirit
who enables us to walk in heaven.

Gospel

At that time Jesus declared, "I thank you, Father, Lord of heaven and earth, that you have hidden these things from the wise and understanding and revealed them to babes; yea, Father, for such was your gracious will. All things have been delivered to me by my Father; and no one knows the Son except the Father, and no one knows the Father except the Son and any one to whom the Son chooses to reveal him. Come to me, all who labor and are heavy laden, and I will give you rest. Take my yoke upon you, and learn from me; for I am gentle and lowly in heart, and you will find rest for your souls" (Mt 11:25-29).

Meditation

We begin to experience ourselves as simple creatures in the midst of other creatures—creatures who have received the immeasurable gift of life, for which we should thank God and others at every moment. Even those who deal us some blows are our benefactors because they help to free us from ourselves. So if we easily brood about unimportant things, let us stop brooding. It is God's will that we free ourselves from such resentment. If we have a tendency toward lying, anger, restlessness or impatience, let us begin to free ourselves from these. If we examine ourselves well, we will find that countless desires fragment us. Now we desire one thing, and immediately we want another. Now we plan one thing, but then change that desire for another. Once a monkey looked at himself in a mirror. He saw something ugly. He snatched the mirror and broke it on the ground. The same thing happens to us. Every fragment of our being, every desire breaks and divides our ego. Our task is to reassemble all these fragments so as to finally have an authentic self. Then we will be able to carry out God's will. We will be truly human only when we successfully replace our endless desires with the will of God. Then we will start on the way to salvation. Christ has not told us to retire to a mountain for thirty or forty years, nor has he told us to be uninterested in matters pertaining to history and life. Instead, he said: *Change your thinking and do the Father's will.* To do the will of the Father means to begin to want what God wants. First, therefore, our purification is absolutely necessary, so that the will of God may descend upon us and make us new creatures, truly human. Therefore, Christ says: *the meek will inherit the earth.*

The meek are those who put up no resistance to the Father's will. They have lost their own will and have made themselves docile instruments in God's hands. They will inherit the earth because they discover the mysterious forces governing the universe and set themselves in harmony with them. Thus, they will possess not only the earth, but the universe. When we are able to fulfill God's will, we immediately become his cooperators, persons who continue the work of salvation and creation that God accomplishes in the universe.[15]

Responsory

v. God will fill your every need
  according to his abundance.
*r. God will fill your every need
  according to his abundance.*
v. It is God who arouses in you
  the desire and the accomplishment,
r. According to his abundance.
v. Glory to the Father, to the Son and to the Holy Spirit.
*r. God will fill your every need
  according to his abundance.*

Intercessions

Let us lift our prayer to God and thank him, for in Christ, risen from the dead, he has given us his very life:

We proclaim the light of the risen Christ.

Grant, O Lord, that with free steps:
—we may move from the threshold of the dawn to the sunset.

We are your free children:
—why do we worry about riches, glory and the power of the mighty?

We could keep or lose roof and garments, bread and gold:
—may our hearts remain steadfast and calm.

Let us go forward, ignoring fear:
—comforted by your free spirit, composing psalms in the name of all creation.

Our wealth is the mystery of God:
—let us proclaim the light of the risen Christ; let us set our hearts on things above.

Prayer

As the flame seeks
its own element in the air,
so our soul seeks you, O Lord,
its only element,
its beginning and final end.
Through Christ our Lord. Amen.

(Sing an appropriate closing hymn.)

Prayer to Mary

(optional)

Then said Mary, the mother,
(who from the threshold gazed afar,
while the yet unborn baby
of the other mother leapt in the womb):

"Yes, peoples will call me blessed:
the Almighty has done great things in me!"
Thank you, O Father, because you have hidden
your secrets from the wise.

The believer believes that God is with the humble,
that the great and the foolish have no future:
that in the divine history the leader
is only the person who is poor and nameless!

Glory be to the Father, to the Son, to the Holy Spirit—
the only God who chooses the weak:
these two mothers now count more
then do all the world's powerful together.

15

Eucharist: "Place" of Communion

Contemplating the Eucharistic mystery, we know, in a true and real way, that the human and divine are indivisibly joined. Neither is overpowered or brought to nothing, but together they form an identity, an identifiable and definite "place" where the desired unity is manifested and energies are multiplied and enhanced. In a pure and perfect form, Christ Jesus continues to incarnate the creative word—a perennial wellspring—with a goodness and beauty that we can now know and enjoy in him. It is therefore fundamental to confidently approach this wellspring and to continue to return to it amid the contradictions of temporal and worldly experiences. Let nothing and no one destroy or even divert this basic feeling in us. Let each of us authentically become a physical "place" for the communion of the divine and human that was instituted by Jesus, the Son of God and son of Mary.

Invitation to Prayer

v. How blessed are they who dwell in your house.
r. Pilgrims who carry your ways in their heart.
v. To the point of inebriation they enjoy good things
r. That enrich your dwelling place.
v. The joyful heart sings in the shadow
r. Of your wings, my Lord and God.

(Sing an appropriate opening hymn.)

Prayer

Lord, help us to attain communion of love
and make you our firm dwelling place.
May nothing in us, conscious or otherwise,
betray this love.
We recognize and greet you
with silent devotion in the breaking of the bread.
You are God, and live and reign with God the Father,
in the unity of the Holy Spirit forever and ever. Amen.

Reading

In the following instructions I do not commend you, because when you come together it is not for the better but for the worse. For, in the first place, when you assemble as a church, I hear that there are divisions among you; and I partly believe it, for there must be factions among you in order that those who are genuine among you may be recognized. When you meet together, it is not the Lord's supper that you eat. For in eating, each one goes ahead with his own meal, and one is hungry and another is drunk. What! Do you not have houses to eat and drink in? Or do you despise the church of God and humiliate those who have nothing? What shall I say to you? Shall I commend you in this? No, I will not (1 Cor 11:17-22).

Psalm 133

How good and pleasant it is
when brothers live together in unity!
It is like precious oil poured on the head,
running down upon the beard,
running down Aaron's beard,
down upon the collar of his robes.
It is as if the dew of Hermon were falling on Mount Zion.
For there the Lord bestows the blessing,
even life forevermore.

Undivided and holy Trinity,
we want to confess you and sing to you:
you are the wellspring of our love,
the goal of our harmony.

Gospel

"Do not think that I have come to bring peace on earth; I have not come to bring peace, but a sword. For I have come to set a man against his father, and a daughter against her mother, and a daughter-in-law against her mother-in-law; and a man's foes will be those of his own household. He who loves father or mother more than me is not worthy of me; and he who loves son or daughter more than me is not worthy of me; and he who does not take his cross and follow me is not worthy of me. He who finds his life will lose it, and he who loses his life for my sake will find it.

"He who receives you receives me, and he who receives me receives him who sent me. He who receives a prophet because he is a prophet shall receive a prophet's reward, and he who receives a righteous man because he is a righteous man shall receive a righteous man's reward. And whoever gives to one of these little ones even a cup of cold water because he is a disciple, truly I say to you, he shall not lose his reward" (Mt 10:34-42).

Meditation

Ever since "in the beginning" God designed a loving plan for humanity, he has unceasingly pronounced the creative and liberating word: "Let us make man in our image, after our likeness" (Gen 1:26). Christ contains the present fullness and future promise of this word made flesh, which, amid the contradictions of history, grows and increases toward the final fulfillment: man-God.

The Gospel never defines humanity: rather Christ relates concrete and precise experiences of it. The parables relate a real landscape of recognizable characters. Christ always wants to encounter the "everyday" person. If there is a reserve, a caution, on his part, it is that of not manifesting his "secret." Until the final days, he hides his mysterious communion with the Father. Without veils and without reserve, he lives his humanity almost as if it were a mirror reflecting each person he meets.

The humanity of Christ is the concrete place—today we say "the theological locus"—in which the mystery of God allows for a one-on-one encounter with the mystery of each person. The totality of God and man are so involved that conventional masks, social differences and racial discriminations—yesterday as today—leap aside, and the living and true person is questioned and called by name. Everyone finds himself naked and defenseless.

The various personal, environmental and historical situations remain only a setting within which the ultimate roots are discovered. Christ always aims at the human "heart," where "secret thoughts are revealed" and everything is always called into question, so that dross, delusions and deceits may fall away and the person may be restored to his or her inner truth: eternal restlessness.

Each person is sought, accepted and loved for what he or she is, and then questioned, shaken up and impelled toward what he or she desires to be and can become. In this sense, there is no privilege and no exclusion. Notwithstanding this, in Christ's life his specific preferences emerge: the little ones, the poor and sinners.[16]

Responsory

v. Whoever remains in me and I in him produces much fruit.
r. Whoever remains in me and I in him produces much fruit.
v. Whoever eats of me abides in me and I in him
r. And produces much fruit.
v. Glory to the Father, to the Son and to the Holy Spirit.
r. Whoever remains in me and I in him produces much fruit.

Intercessions

We pray to you, Holy Spirit, who are the love of the Father and the Son. Inflame our hearts as we pray:

O Spirit, dwell in us.

O Holy Spirit, free our lives from evil:
—and transfigure them in your fire of love.

O Spirit, grant that in you we may be what we really are:
—break our selfish barriers, transform us into the reality of communion.

Make us aware that you live in us, your temples:
—that your presence may illumine our flesh with utter beauty.

Keep pride and the arrogance of indifference far from us:
—enlarge our hearts to embrace the whole truth.

O love without sunrise or sunset:
—deliver us, your pilgrim creatures, from harshness and intolerance, from all lack of understanding and self-alienation.

O love, you gather all into one:
—deliver us, your upward-bound creatures, from all factions and divisions, from every hostility and separation.

With your presence always reveal new creatures to love; show us the profound reasons for the lives of all:
—break down the boundaries of our selfish egos to the point of perfect communion; immerse us in the intoxicating wave of your joy.

Prayer

O Lord, we want to be one bread with you.
Help us to understand
that the only important thing
is to identify ourselves more and more with you.
Unite our being
with your absolute being;
to be always stronger,
calmer and more disinterested
within your loving will.
You are God, and live and reign forever and ever. Amen.

(Sing an appropriate closing hymn.)

Prayer to Mary

(optional)

Will the miracle still be possible—
this wonderful exchange of love?
To be the earth that welcomes the Spirit
—to conceive the Word ourselves!

At least you believed, Mary!
We have been wearied by many fables;
troubling idols invade our hearts:
may your faith guide us to the light!

"O children, listen and you will be blessed:
it is the Wisdom of God speaking to you,
a God who watches at the door of your heart
and only waits for each one to open to him.

Blessed are all who follow the way
and are always listening:
those who discover God will have life
and obtain his salvation!"

16

Eucharist: Perfection of the Saints

Bread and wine are basic elements of nourishment and enhance the quality of any meal.

It is the same when we ourselves are viewed in the light of the Eucharistic mystery. We make ourselves into a pure white table, so to speak, on which we place our simple reality so that it may be "sanctified."

The bread is matter that, leavened by God's merciful love, takes on a new form, transfigured by the "fullness" of God that it contains. And the wine is the generous simplicity, the sincere clarity that gifts our spirit with joy and deep meaning. It does not sour our heart with superficial and fleeting satisfactions, nor sadden our soul with disappointing passions.

The Eucharist is the illuminating and fruitful strength of the Spirit, leading us to overcome the tempting obstacles of moralistic adaptations to exterior realities, so that we may be in a "holy" way the ever more transparent image of the perfection of God.

Invitation to Prayer

v. Lord, great is your gentleness.
r. It overflows upon those who take refuge in you.
v. Delightful are the things you have given me;
r. My heritage is splendid indeed.
v. I give you thanks: you have worked marvels for me,
r. O admirable author of wonders.

(Sing an appropriate opening hymn.)

Prayer

O provident and holy God,
you have sent from heaven
the true bread that sustains us
on our difficult journey toward the holy mountain
and the drink that quenches
the thirst of the endless wait.
Grant that, strengthened in body and in spirit,
we may become untiring imitators of your perfect love.
Through our Lord Jesus Christ, your Son, who is God
and lives and reigns with you in the unity of the Holy Spirit
forever and ever. Amen.

Reading

For this reason I bow my knees before the Father, from whom every family in heaven and on earth is named, that according to the riches of his glory he may grant you to be strengthened with might through his Spirit in the inner man, and that Christ may dwell in your hearts through faith; that you, being rooted and grounded in love, may have power to comprehend with all the saints what is the breadth and length and height and depth, and to know the love of Christ which surpasses knowledge, that you may be filled with all the fullness of God (Eph 3:14-19).

Psalm 146

Praise the Lord.
Praise the Lord, O my soul.
I will praise the Lord all my life;
I will sing praise to my God as long as I live.
Do not put your trust in princes, in mortal men, who cannot save.
When their spirit departs, they return to the ground;
on that very day their plans come to nothing.
Blessed is he whose help is the God of Jacob,
whose hope is in the Lord his God,
the Maker of heaven and earth,
the sea, and everything that is in them—
the Lord, who remains faithful forever.
He upholds the cause of the oppressed
and gives food to the hungry.
The Lord sets prisoners free, the Lord gives sight to the blind,
the Lord lifts up those who are bowed down,
the Lord loves the righteous.
The Lord watches over the alien,
and sustains the fatherless and the widow,
but he frustrates the way of the wicked.
The Lord reigns forever,
your God, O Zion, for all generations.

Praise the Lord.
To him, the Lord sent by the Father
to inaugurate the temple of grace, let all victims sing glory
in the certainty that the kingdom is coming.

Gospel

And behold, one came up to him, saying, "Teacher, what good deed must I do, to have eternal life?" And he said to him, "Why do you ask me about what is good? One there is who is good. If you would enter life, keep the commandments." He said to him, "Which?" And Jesus said, "You shall not kill, You shall not commit adultery, You shall not steal, You shall not bear false witness, Honor your father and mother, and, You shall love your neighbor as yourself." The young man said to him, "All these I have observed; what do I still lack?" Jesus said to him, "If you would be perfect, go, sell what you possess and give to the poor, and you will have treasure in heaven; and come, follow me." When the young man heard this he went away sorrowful; for he had great possessions (Mt 19:16-22).

Meditation

"Pure simplicity" opens the heart to faith and its realities, without letting its expansion be impeded by doubts, uncertainties or torments that arise from reason or established habits. Simplicity easily leads the heart to the goal of love and binds hearts in unfailing communion:

"To see Christ! That is the heart's most ardent longing. O, Jesus! I venerate your face hidden beneath the appearance of Bread. Grant that one day, the veil may be removed, and I might freely contemplate you in heaven!

"This is the vision of Jesus, of his uniqueness, of his innocence and passion to the end along the journey of purification.

"In memory of him, I look for him under the veil of bread.

"I look for him under the veil of the Gospel, where the rays of light free the soul from its prison and from the darkness that makes it vacillating and uncertain.

"I look for him under the veil of innocence, in children; under the veil of the Passion, in the sufferings and self-denial of my brothers and sisters.

"I look for him under the veil of mother nature: the wheat..., the lamb..., the stone, the wood, the thorns.... Each creature is marked with his seal and reveals, as it were, a ray of his invisible beauty. Yes, I look for Christ along the way. But one's soul must be open to recognizing him, to seeing him.

"It is my soul that gives me sight—not my eyes. And it is clarity that makes the soul able to see, ready to see. What is clarity? It is pure simplicity, it is sincerity, it is constancy on the right path."[17]

Responsory

v. In the image of the Holy One who called you
become holy yourselves in all your conduct.
*r. In the image of the Holy One who called you
become holy yourselves in all your conduct.*
v. Therefore, be perfect.
r. Become holy yourselves in all your conduct.
v. Glory to the Father and to the Son and to the Holy Spirit.
*r. In the image of the Holy One who called you
become holy yourselves in all your conduct.*

Intercessions

We pray untiringly, interceding for all our brothers and sisters, and we ask:

Lord, hear our prayer.

O Father, you love us with a boundless love:
—break down our selfish barriers and transform us into a loving presence.

O Father, you are the origin of everything that exists and the goal toward which all creation tends:
—make us aware that our lives are marked by your seal and that you lead everything to your perfection.

Lord Jesus Christ, at times we grow weary of believing in the mystery of your complete humanity:
—confirm our weak faith and help us always to discover your face in the faces of our brothers and sisters.

Lord Jesus Christ, you are light for all who seek and accept you:
—enlighten our hearts, so we can follow you along the path you trod in obedience to the Father.

O Holy Spirit, final gift of the Son made flesh, you dwell within us and lead us to the kingdom:
—give us the strength to resist the seductions of the evil one, so that we do not obscure the light of your presence within us.

O Holy Spirit, you urge us always toward wider horizons in the mystery of the encounter with God in time:
—enable us to recognize in every person a brother or sister whom the Father loves and for whom the Lord Jesus gave his life.

Prayer

O God, you are not far away,
but always beyond all our knowing
and all our feeling.
Let us not be frightened
by the limits of human experience;

grant instead that we may understand
with an austere awareness
that you reveal yourself to us
in the simplicity of our service.
Through Christ our Lord. Amen.

(Sing an appropriate closing hymn.)

Prayer to Mary

(optional)

You are the palm of Kadesh, Mary,
an enclosed garden, a holy dwelling,
always bearing your holy fruit,
now radiantly hovering over the world.

You are the cathedral of great silence,
a ring of gold linking us with the Eternal,
joining the spaces that cannot be joined,
like a bridge spanning our exile.

Mother of glory, now you are the image
of what his Church will be one day:
the bride adorned and ready for the wedding,
the holy city descending from heaven.

But you already give us your Son
because alone we are lost
and have no more reason to live.

O Trinity, mysterious and blessed,
we praise you because you have given us
the new dawn that announces your day,
Christ, the glory of all creation.

17

Eucharist:
Proclamation of Transfiguration

The mystery we contemplate in the Eucharistic bread and wine recalls what is present in seed within each person and awaits full revelation. This is the absolute "newness" brought about in humanity by Jesus Christ and then given to each person who approaches this "throne of grace" with confident openness. It is the united action of the Father, who chooses persons out of love and gives holiness and purity to our fragile and dark condition; of the Son, who enables us to know the mystery of God's will in listening to his word; of the Spirit, who makes all things new and is the seal of truth transforming us into the image of a child of glory. It is necessary to descend silently into our depths, enlightened by the Spirit, to become actively aware and faithfully announce in word and action what is said from on high to each person: "You are my son, I have begotten you."

Invitation to Prayer

v. The Lord is a shield and sun.
r. God gives grace and glory.
v. Your garments are magnificence and splendor.
r. You are robed as with a mantle of light.
v. Lord, you truly are my light.
*r. My God, you are splendor
that brings my darkness to daylight.*

(Sing an appropriate opening hymn.)

Prayer

O Lord, marvelous friend,
invisible guest at our table,
pervade our entire being and transfigure it.
You alone live in us and with us.
To you, in the unity of the Father
and of the Holy Spirit,
be glory forever and ever. Amen.

Reading

Blessed be the God and Father of our Lord Jesus Christ, who has blessed us in Christ with every spiritual blessing in the heavenly places, even as he chose us in him before the foundation of the world, that we should be holy and blameless before him. He destined us in love to be his sons through Jesus Christ, according to the purpose of his will, to the praise of his glorious grace which he freely bestowed on us in the Beloved. In him we have redemption through his blood, the forgiveness of our trespasses, according to the riches of his grace which he lavished upon us. For he has

Eucharist: Proclamation of Transfiguration

made known to us in all wisdom and insight the mystery of his will, according to his purpose which he set forth in Christ as a plan for the fullness of time, to unite all things in him, things in heaven and things on earth.

In him, according to the purpose of him who accomplishes all things according to the counsel of his will, we who first hoped in Christ have been destined and appointed to live for the praise of his glory. In him you also, who have heard the word of truth, the gospel of your salvation, and have believed in him, were sealed with the promised Holy Spirit, who is the guarantee of our inheritance until we acquire possession of it, to the praise of his glory (Eph 1:3-14).

Psalm 8

O Lord, our Lord,
how majestic is your name in all the earth!
You have set your glory above the heavens.
From the lips of children and infants
you have ordained praise
because of your enemies,
to silence the foe and the avenger.
When I consider your heavens,
the work of your fingers,
the moon and the stars,
which you have set in place;
what is man that you are mindful of him,
the son of man that you care for him?
You made him a little lower than the heavenly beings
and crowned him with glory and honor.
You made him ruler over the works of your hands;

you put everything under his feet:
all flocks and herds,
and the beasts of the field,
the birds of the air,
and the fish of the sea,
all that swim the paths of the seas.
O Lord, our Lord,
how majestic is your name in all the earth!

Glory to the Father in the highest heavens,
glory to the Son, his eternal splendor,
and to the Spirit, heart of the world:
even to humanity, his image, be glory.

Gospel

After six days Jesus took with him Peter and James and John, and led them up a high mountain apart by themselves; and he was transfigured before them, and his garments became glistening, intensely white, as no fuller on earth could bleach them. And there appeared to them Elijah with Moses; and they were talking to Jesus. And Peter said to Jesus, "Master, it is well that we are here; let us make three booths, one for you and one for Moses and one for Elijah." For he did not know what to say, for they were exceedingly afraid. And a cloud overshadowed them, and a voice came out of the cloud, "This is my beloved Son; listen to him." And suddenly looking around they no longer saw anyone with them but Jesus only.

And as they were coming down the mountain, he charged them to tell no one what they had seen, until the Son of man should have risen from the dead. So they kept the matter to themselves, questioning what the rising from the dead meant (Mk 9:2-10).

Meditation

Why are we so hesitant to accept as an essential component of human nature our longing to return to Unity, our dream of a love without illusions?

Why are the pathways of this divided world so alluring; why do we retrace them even when they have given us only empty hands and broken hearts?

The words of the Gospel make our desire more ardent: "I in them and you [Father] in me, that they may become perfectly one" (Jn 17:23).

The reed flute moans, dreaming of the stalk from which it was hewn. Its music is nostalgia for the song of the water where it grew, for the rustle of the wind that softly and strongly played with it, for the warmth of the sun that changed its garments into gold.

The flesh, dreaming of the Spirit that gave it life, passionately begs for a kiss, craving the supreme ecstasy.

The mind, tired of its small calculations, abandons itself like a bride to the ardor of a thought that knows no restrictions and limitations.

The heart repeats: always beyond, always beyond is the dwelling of the Beloved, the fullness of Unity. Deceived and embittered by desertion, the fleeting loves of earth are like smoky fires that separate and pollute. The heart wants a love that consumes it in the fullness of union.

Our human work is to reconcile heaven and earth within ourselves—transforming flesh into spirit, fusing in the fire of Unity the elements which compose us; transmuting our earthly bread into the Bread come down from heaven.

Let us live in preparation for the supreme unification.

Let us not do anything that does not prepare us for that encounter, that does not transfigure our humble reality.

Let us live with a pure and peaceful will, in harmony with the supreme aspiration of our being: the fullness of Unity.

Opening to the infinite dimension of the Absence, the self will celebrate the truth and life of the Bread come down from heaven to revivify earthly bread and make possible its transfiguration.[18]

Responsory

v. You have clothed us anew
with full knowledge, in the image of our Creator.
r. You have clothed us anew
with full knowledge, in the image of our Creator.
v. Desire to be clothed with the heavenly body,
r. With full knowledge, in the image of your creator.
v. Glory to the Father, to the Son and to the Holy Spirit.
r. You have clothed us anew
with full knowledge, in the image of our Creator.

Intercessions

Let us pray to the Lord Jesus Christ, the light who illumines every being that comes into existence, and let us say:

Illumine our night, Lord.

O Christ, before going to Jerusalem to fulfill the Father's plan, you revealed yourself to the apostles with the glory of the resurrection:
—grant that the Church may never weaken in her certitude that you have conquered the prince of the darkness.
O Christ, on Tabor the Father presented you to humanity as the revealer of the Word of life:

—grant that we may always listen to your voice and follow you on the path you have marked out before us.

O Christ, you are the beginning and the end of all existence, the first-born of every creature and of those risen from the dead:
—grant that we may share in your divine life, as children whom the Father loves.

O Christ, in the glory of your transfiguration we have known the great destiny to which the Father has called us:
—transform us in the depths of our being, so that we may always be more like you.

O Christ, all creation awaits the fulfillment of time and the dawning of your day that will have no sunset:
—together with the Spirit dwelling within us, we pray you to come soon and lead us into your kingdom of joy and peace.

Prayer

O Lord, we desire the fulfillment
of the impossible dream of life that you enkindle within us.
To know you, to possess you, to be one with you,
while immersed in our human condition;
to transform the twilight glimmer in our minds
into the fullness of your light;
to attain endless peace and joy
amid earthly tensions and sufferings;
to establish endless freedom
in a mechanistic world;
to discover and attain immortal life
in a fragile and mortal body.
Through Christ our Lord. Amen.

(Sing an appropriate closing hymn.)

Prayer to Mary

(optional)

The command was to await the Spirit:
so they all kept vigil together.
Did you perhaps lead the prayer,
as he did at the last supper?

Surely the prophet saw you at the beginning
when the Spirit adorned creation,
when the struggle with the serpent began,
and then during the ark's long journey.

Surely you were the promised land
the island of the holy landing-field,
where the Spirit had already descended
to make you fruitful with the divine seed.

Be present with us till the last days:
the same wind now shakes the house,
the same fire of Horeb blazes
and opens the way in the new desert!

18

Eucharist: Proclamation of Glory

Ideally, the altar is the center of a cosmos formed by the curved apse behind it, or the focal point of every location within the church, which attracts the awed attention of each believer. Upon it are bread and a chalice of wine. Recently the bread and wine did not exist; now they do, through the collaboration of various agents. They are products of human creativity and labor and the technology that human beings possess. Freed from every earthly bond, they share in all reality. They have been set apart to be sanctified.

The believer sees and knows that upon this very place God descends with all his glory (his real and active presence) through the mediation of humble gestures and simple words. This is not an individual opinion, but universal knowledge.

Likewise, the believer is carried out of self, stripped of nonessentials and placed in the light of life's simple truth. Altars that have a tomblike shape recall the detachment from self that seals every self-offering.

At the same time, the believer perceives that a real power transforms him or her; one returns to the world with a new being—a living proclamation of the fullness that sustains one in struggle and in hope. Activity is again clothed in glorious meaning.

Invitation to Prayer

v. The just will flourish like palm trees,
r. Like cedars of Lebanon, they will grow tall.
v. They will enter the presence of God
r. In the meadows of life.
v. I will sing of victory in the tents of God.
r. I will dance and chant hymns of praise to my Lord.

(Sing an appropriate opening hymn.)

Prayer

O Father,
you have manifested your infinite wisdom
in what our mortal eyes
consider a scandal and folly.
Enable us to understand and live
the mystery of the cross as the way for us to meet you.
May your Son Jesus Christ live in us
and make us new creatures in the Spirit,
an anticipation and promise of your day of glory.
He is God, and lives and reigns with you
in the unity of the Holy Spirit forever and ever. Amen.

Reading

If then you have been raised with Christ, seek the things that are above, where Christ is, seated at the right hand of God. Set your mind on things that are above, not on things that are on earth. For you have died, and your life is hid with Christ in God. When Christ who is our life appears, then you also will appear with him in glory (Col 3:1-4).

Psalm 24

The earth is the Lord's, and everything in it,
the world, and all who live in it;
for he founded it upon the seas
and established it upon the waters.
Who may ascend the hill of the Lord?
Who may stand in his holy place?
He who has clean hands and a pure heart,
who does not lift up his soul to an idol,
or swear by what is false.
He will receive blessing from the Lord
and vindication from God his Savior.
Such is the generation of those who seek him,
who seek your face, O God of Jacob.
Lift up your heads, O you gates;
be lifted up, you ancient doors,
that the King of glory may come in.
Who is this King of glory?
The Lord strong and mighty,
the Lord mighty in battle.
Lift up your heads, O you gates;
lift them up, you ancient doors,
that the King of glory may come in.
Who is he, this King of glory?
The Lord Almighty—
he is the King of glory.

Glory to the Father, to the Son and to the Holy Spirit,
as it was in the beginning,
is now and will be forever, amen!

Gospel

"I do not pray for these only, but also for those who believe in me through their word, that they may all be one; even as you, Father, are in me, and I in you, that they also may be in us, so that the world may believe that you have sent me. The glory which you have given me I have given to them, that they may be one even as we are one. I in them and you in me, that they may become perfectly one, so that the world may know that you have sent me and have loved them even as you have loved me. Father, I desire that they also, whom you have given me, may be with me where I am, to behold my glory which you have given me in your love for me before the foundation of the world. O righteous Father, the world has not known you, but I have known you; and these know that you have sent me. I made known to them your name, and I will make it known, that the love with which you have loved me may be in them, and I in them" (Jn 17:20-26).

Meditation

Human hope cannot avoid the "ultimate questions" that lead to the proclamation of hope in Christ. According to Scripture, hope is the projection of faith into history, "the assurance of things hoped for, the conviction of things not seen" (Heb 11:1).

Personal life and universal history are entrusted to the "promise" of the Father, who in his Christ has revealed and brought about "hope against hope."

Hope, then, is founded on the certitude that God remains faithful. He is *within* events and guides them *onward* with patience and perseverance.

The God of Christ is not absent from history. He neither precedes nor follows our daily historical exodus toward the land of ultimate freedom. *He is the future in the present.* The resurrection of Christ is already the future that unites the glory of humanity and the glory of God. It reveals itself and works within the here-and-nowness of each event.

"Fear not, little flock, for it is your Father's good pleasure to give you the kingdom" (Lk 12:32). "I have overcome the world" (Jn 16:33). "This is the victory that overcomes the world, our faith" (1 Jn 5:4).

It is upon these words that the believer places his or her "bet" in and with history—to wait and at the same time to be ready for God's "surprise."[19]

Responsory

v. The God of all grace has called you to his glory.
r. *The God of all grace has called you to his glory.*
v. You groan inwardly, awaiting adoption as children.
r. *He has called you to his glory.*
v. Glory to the Father, to the Son and to the Holy Spirit.
r. *The God of all grace has called you to his glory.*

Intercessions

We pray to the Holy Spirit, the final gift of the Son made flesh, that he may live in us and make us children of the heavenly Father. So we pray:

Spirit, set us on fire with your love.

Come, O Spirit of fire:
—reveal to us the new life that you cause to flower on the earth.
Guide us to the maturity of love:
—gently and strongly, like grain ripening in the fields.

Shatter the fear that separates earth from heaven:
—help us to understand that earth is your cherished dwelling, that joy and light are bestowed upon the hearts of all.

Help us to realize that we are not born to accomplish limited deeds, to enclose ourselves within small spaces
—but to be illumined with your light and to transmit the transforming word of redemption.

Grant, O Spirit, that it not be useless to turn our eyes to heaven to seek perfection:
—teach us that perfection is not only above or beyond, but has come down to us and is diffused with sweet insistence within the human heart.

Teach us that here on earth, in each of us, in all our brothers and sisters, in every creature:
—your meek and powerful presence lives and acts.

Strengthen in our minds, O Spirit, the most human certitude that we have, and which makes us all one:
—our aspirations for peace, for joy, for love, for life.

Prayer

Father,
we want to believe in what is,
not in appearances;
to believe in the Spirit,
who takes shape in matter;
to believe in the divine seed in the human heart
that awaits the resurrection;
to believe in the divine kingdom,
toward which the human kingdom tends;

to believe that faith is a certainty,
even though we do not understand it.
Through Christ our Lord. Amen.

(Sing an appropriate closing hymn.)

Prayer to Mary

(optional)

"A great sign appeared in the sky:
the Woman clothed with the sun;
she held the moon under her feet
and a crown of stars on her head.

"She still bore her son in her womb
and cried and suffered the pains of birth!
Then a terrible monster appeared
with seven heads and seven diadems.

"It shattered the vast sky with its tail,
and a third of the stars fell to the ground;
then the dragon stood in front of the woman,
ready to destroy the fruit of her womb.

"Now with eagle wings the woman
was taken away to the desert by God"—
to give birth to him, Mother, return:
through you, hope comes back to the earth!

Notes

[1] Primo Mazzolari, *La pasqua*, Vicenza: La Locusta, 1982, pp. 46-48.

[2] Giovanni Vannucci, *Fate questo in memoria di me*, in "Servitium" I, n. 20/21 (1971), p. 412. Reprinted in *Pellegrino dell'Assoluto*, CENS: Liscate, 1985, p. 158.

[3] Giovanni Vannucci, *Il mistero dell'alimentazione*, in "Servitium" III, n. 21 (1982), pp. 37-38.

[4] Silvano Fausti, *La morte di Gesù come martirio*, in "Servitium" III, n. 16/17 (1981), p. 34.

[5] G. Bruni, *Dall'eucaristia domenicale alla vita quotidiana*, in "Servitium" III, n. 4 (1979), p. 45.

[6] David Maria Turoldo, *Eucaristia, segreta aspirazione dell'umanità*, in "Servitium" III, n. 25 (1983), pp. 29-30.

[7] G. Vannucci, *Simbolo e linguaggio*, in "Servitium" I, n. 20/21 (1871), pp. 380-381. Reprinted in *Pellegrino dell'Assoluto*, CENS: Liscate, 1985, pp. 144-145.

[8] L.M. Chauvet, *Linguaggio e simbolo*, Turin, 1982.

[9] Silvano Maggiani, *Dal pane all'eucaristia al pane*, in "Servitium," III, n. 21 (1982), pp. 80-82.

[10] Dimitri Staniloae, *Le preghiera in un mondo secolarizzato*, in "Servitium," III, n. 13 (1981), pp. 35-38.

[11] David Maria Turoldo, *Due aspetti di un solo ideale*, in "Il Cenacolo," 64 (February 1987) 2, p. 20.

[12] A. Levi, *"L'al di là" del regno di Dio*, in "Servitium" II, n. 5 (1974), pp. 683-688.

[13] Giancarlo Bruni, *Dalla creazione a "quel riposo,"* in "Servitium," III, n. 57 (1988), pp. 37-38.

[14] Giancarlo Bruni, *Dall'eucaristia alla vita*, in "Servitium," III, n. 4 (1979), pp. 45-46.

[15] Giovanni Vannucci, *La volontà del Padre*, in *Libertà dello spirito*, CENS 1985, pp. 264-265.

[16] Umberto Vivarelli, *Come Cristo incontra l'uomo* in "Servitium", II, n. 1 (1974), pp. 32-33.

[17] Giovanni Vannucci, *La via della pura semplicità*, *Libertà dello spirito*, CENS 1985, pp. 245-246.

[18] Giovanni Vannucci, *Il camino verso l'incontro*, in *Pellegrino dell'Assoluto*, CENS, 1985, pp. 284-285.

[19] Umberto Vivareli, *La speranza ultima*, in "Servitum", II, n. 5 (1974), pp. 661-662.

Pauline BOOKS & MEDIA

ALASKA
 750 West 5th Ave., Anchorage, AK 99501; 907-272-8183

CALIFORNIA
 3908 Sepulveda Blvd., Culver City, CA 90230; 310-397-8676
 5945 Balboa Ave., San Diego, CA 92111; 619-565-9181
 46 Geary Street, San Francisco, CA 94108; 415-781-5180

FLORIDA
 145 S.W. 107th Ave., Miami, FL 33174; 305-559-6715

HAWAII
 1143 Bishop Street, Honolulu, HI 96813; 808-521-2731

ILLINOIS
 172 North Michigan Ave., Chicago, IL 60601; 312-346-4228

LOUISIANA
 4403 Veterans Memorial Blvd., Metairie, LA 70006; 504-887-7631

MASSACHUSETTS
 50 St. Paul's Ave., Jamaica Plain, Boston, MA 02130; 617-522-8911
 Rte. 1, 885 Providence Hwy., Dedham, MA 02026; 617-326-5385

MISSOURI
 9804 Watson Rd., St. Louis, MO 63126; 314-965-3512

NEW JERSEY
 561 U.S. Route 1, Wick Plaza, Edison, NJ 08817; 908-572-1200

NEW YORK
 150 East 52nd Street, New York, NY 10022; 212-754-1110
 78 Fort Place, Staten Island, NY 10301; 718-447-5071

OHIO
 2105 Ontario Street, Cleveland, OH 44115; 216-621-9427

PENNSYLVANIA
 Northeast Shopping Center, 9171-A Roosevelt Blvd., Philadelphia, PA 19114; 215-676-9494

SOUTH CAROLINA
 243 King Street, Charleston, SC 29401; 803-577-0175

TENNESSEE
 4811 Poplar Ave., Memphis, TN 38117; 901-761-2987

TEXAS
 114 Main Plaza, San Antonio, TX 78205; 210-224-8101

VIRGINIA
 1025 King Street, Alexandria, VA 22314; 703-549-3806

CANADA
 3022 Dufferin Street, Toronto, Ontario, Canada M6B 3T5; 416-781-9131